ORGANISATION DEVELOPMENT IN HEALTH CARE

In memory of Professor Mo Malek, 1949-2001

Professor Mo Malek – 1949–2001 – A Dedication

This text is dedicated to Professor Mo Malek, Professor of Health Care Policy, Planning and Management at the University of St Andrews, and founder of the *Strategic Issues in Health Care Management* (SIHCM) conferences. Sadly, Mo passed away on 12 March 2001 after a short illness. Our thoughts are with his family, especially his wife Linda, and children Rebecca, Ali, Miriam and Gemma. Mo went to school in Switzerland and obtained his first degree, in economics, at the University of Tehran. He taught in Iran for a couple of years before coming to Queen Mary College of London University, first as a postgraduate student, then research assistant, then temporary lecturer. Mo moved to St Andrews in 1981, as a Lecturer in Economics, being promoted to Reader in 1991, and being awarded a Chair in Health Policy, Planning and Management in 1995.

Mo contributed much, both internationally and across disciplines. However, it is perhaps for his work in pharmacoeconomics that he is best known, much of it conducted through the PharmacoEconomics Research Centre (PERC), which he founded and directed. For many people though, it is through the SIHCM conferences that Mo was first encountered.

Mo organised the first SIHCM conference in 1993. Further meetings followed in 1994 (on the theme of *Setting Priorities in Health Care*), 1998 (*Managing Quality, Controlling Costs*) and 2000 (*Efficiency, Quality and Access in Health Care*). Mo's work continues after him as the fifth meeting is planned for April 2002 (on *Policy, Finance and Performance in Health Care*).

Throughout these meetings many hundreds of people from dozens of countries encountered Mo's great hospitality and warmth. The SIHCM meetings were a source of some pride for Mo, and he delighted in the eclectic mix of disciplines and cultures in attendance. He was also concerned that as many as possible should be given a chance to share their work – and many a delegate gave their first ever conference presentation at an SIHCM meeting.

Mo was a tireless worker for his subject area, his institution, and his colleagues. He cared greatly about the development of health care and the appropriate use of health technologies, especially in developing nations. It is with great sadness that we record his death; and it is to his boundless energy, enthusiasm and generosity that this text, which explores some of these issues, is dedicated.

Huw Davies, Manouche Tavakoli, Rosemary Rushmer
SIHCM editors

Organisation Development in Health Care

Strategic issues in health care management

Edited by
ROSEMARY K. RUSHMER, HUW T.O. DAVIES,
MANOUCHE TAVAKOLI AND MO MALEK

Ashgate

Aldershot • Burlington USA • Singapore • Sydney

Published by
Ashgate Publishing Limited
Gower House
Croft Road
Aldershot
Hants GU11 3HR
England

Ashgate Publishing Company
131 Main Street
Burlington, VT 05401-5600 USA

Ashgate website: http://www.ashgate.com

British Library Cataloguing in Publication Data
Organisation development in health care : strategic issues
   in health care management
   1.Health services administration - Congresses
   2.Organizational change - Congresses 3.Strategic planning -
   Congresses
   I.Rushmer, R. K. II.Davies, H. T. O. III.Tavakoli, Manouche
   362.1'068

Library of Congress Control Number: 2001096523

ISBN 0 7546 1611 8

Printed and bound by Athenaeum Press, Ltd.,
Gateshead, Tyne & Wear.

Contents

List of Figures

List of Tables and Boxes

Acknowledgements

We wish to thank, first of all, participants in the Fourth International Conference on *Strategic Issues in Health Care Management* held at the University of St Andrews, Scotland in spring 2000. Over 20 countries were represented from many disciplines, and this eclectic mix ensured rich and varied debates on the problems facing health care as we enter the new millennium. Special thanks go to our plenary speakers, Professors Andrew Bindman and Thomas Rundall from the University of California (in San Francisco, and at Berkeley, respectively), and Sir David Carter, Chief Medical Officer at The Scottish Executive. Their contributions, which both opened and closed the conference, set the tone for some thoughtful discussions throughout. In addition, we are particularly grateful to the session chairs, manuscript reviewers and contributors for their efforts in shaping the material in this volume.

Appreciation is also due to our colleagues in the Department of Management, and the School of Social Sciences, at the University of St Andrews. We are likewise grateful for the excellent support provided by Reprographics, Printing, and Residential and Business Services at St Andrews. These capable and friendly people assisted in preparing conference materials and ensured the smooth running of the conference. Central to the conference planning and management was our conference secretary, Claire Topping. Claire performed wonders before, during and after the meeting, for which we are eternally grateful. In addition, Mehran Zabihollah, Eli Brock, Barbara Lessels and Liz Brodie also contributed to the conference management, and we thank them for their assistance.

Finally, Pat FitzGerald contributed great skill and considerable patience in the preparation of the text, and our publishers Ashgate greatly smoothed the production process: we thank them both.

Of course, none of the above can be held responsible for the final product. Responsibility for the presence of any errors or omissions lies solely with the editors and the contributing authors.

Huw Davies
Manouche Tavakoli
Mo Malek
Rosemary Rushmer

Editors' Preface:
Organisation Development
in Health Care

Introduction

The *Fourth International Conference* on *Strategic Issues in Health Care Management* took place in St Andrews in spring 2000. Delegates from over 20 countries heard around 100 presentations on a diverse range of topics – from the big issues of national health systems reform, to the human problems of developing a patient-focused culture. The result of those three days intense activity was not only new friends and expanding professional networks, but also three eclectic collections of papers on key issues facing health services development: managing quality; developing organisations; and controlling costs. The papers in this volume, selected from nearly 100 original high quality submissions, reflect the upsurge of innovative work currently taking place on *organisation development issues within health care*. Papers in companion volumes examine health policy issues from an economic perspective (*Health Policy and Economics: Strategic Issues in Health Care Management*, Ashgate, 2001), and the challenges of quality in health care (*Quality in Health Care: Strategic Issues in Health Care Management*, Ashgate, 2001).

What is Organisation Development?

At the beginning of this volume it is perhaps worth summarising the main aims behind an organisation development (OD) perspective to organisational change. The main belief of an OD approach is that the methods and findings of the social sciences can be applied to an organisational setting to create an organisational environment that will foster and facilitate an excellent performance by its members. Logically, this rests on the assumption that the members of the organisation are *able* to improve practice (given the right conditions), thus training and individual development are cornerstones of the approach. Great attention is paid to the way people and services are organised in order to achieve the set tasks, in what functional groups and with what supporting infrastructures. The argument is that a structure and climate that allows professionals to actively participate in the provision and organisation of their service will give rise to commitment, loyalty, dedication and job satisfaction on the part on the staff. A happy worker is a 'productive worker'. Thus, a unitarist culture is assumed – i.e. that staff will *want* to enhance performance and service delivery (given the opportunity) and that there is a high degree of agreement in what the organisation's purpose is (and how to achieve it).

Readers familiar with the NHS in the UK, may well hear echoes in these assumptions of the term the *NHS family* and, more widely, the strongly held belief that working in health is a vocational undertaking engaged in by like-minded individuals dedicated to providing the best possible care to the patients they serve. Some of these assumptions are addressed and challenged either directly or indirectly by the following papers.

Involvement and Partnership Arrangements

To begin this collection of papers, the first section addresses issues of cooperative working arrangements – what are the best ways to organise staff to encourage cooperation, and avoid duplication and inter-professional rivalry. Changes, driven by legislation, have been introduced as recently as April 1999, aimed at changing the macro-organisational structure of the NHS in the UK. Opening with the paper by Lawrence Benson and Gillian Wright of Bradford, an initial exploration of the introduction of Primary Care Groups (PCG) into England is undertaken. As a form of collaborative working arrangements imposed upon the organisation of health care, the impact, effectiveness and perception of *institutionalised collaboration* by those involved in the groups themselves is mapped out.

The paper by Stephanie Williams pursues this theme by examining the establishment of Local Health Groups in Wales. She concludes that the rationale and theory behind the introduction of collaborative working in Primary Care is sound and commendable but that in practice, implementing hybrid organisational arrangements and structures in practice brings challenges as well as opportunities.

Alternatively, the approach taken by the paper authored by Sue Phillips, Oliver Nyumbu and Brian Toner is to argue that collaborative arrangements and involvement *must* become a working reality. Taking an unashamedly unitarist perspective towards their work in Birmingham, they argue that involvement in change is pivotal in order that health professionals may embrace the changes necessary to allow the organisation to move forwards successfully and adapt to the realities and constraints of service delivery in the new millennium.

Teams and Interdisciplinary Working

Teamworking as an OD technique within health care offers the promise of integrating the differing contribution of the various health professionals in a complementary way to enhance service delivery to patients. A cohesive, loyal unit dedicated to one aspect of service delivery logically can enhance task identity, encourage cooperation and participation and effective working relationships. Given a degree of self-management and autonomy the team can become a concentrated unit of organisational change and best practice.

Rosemary Rushmer, Julia Parker and Sheila Phillips, in their paper, outline details of a change programme in the East of Scotland to introduce self-directed Primary Care Teams. Aiming to foster empowerment, encourage integrated working and reduce duplication, multidisciplinary practice-based teams can localise their service provision to suit the needs of their practice population. However, limits to the degree of local diversity in service provision are outlined as the coherence and consistency of the NHS is potentially threatened, and health care dictated by postcode looms.

Brain O'Neill and colleagues, working in a Canadian context, argue convincingly for the benefits of interdisciplinary training as a basis for building future cooperative relationships. They argue that interprofessional education brings unique benefits, widening the learning experience by bringing to the fore the multidisciplinary concerns involved in the treatment of chronic, complex and infectious diseases such as HIV/AIDS.

Similarly, Terry Downes and Jayne Sayers examine the efficacy of teamworking as a means to integrate and coordinate the delivery of care to the elderly with mental health problems in the Birmingham area. They map the success of a newly-formed team of five liaison nurses facilitating the multidisciplinary care needed to manage the complex social and health needs of these elderly individuals and their families.

Leadership

Pursuing the organisational problem of coordination and integration, commonality of purpose and focus in the organisation of health care services can be provided not just by integrating structures or by teamworking, but also by and through effective organisational leadership. The visionary leader can be a powerful focus in creating and disseminating the dominant organisation ethic and stabilising a unitarist culture.

Helen Bussell and colleagues in Middlesborough investigate the skills necessary in order to fulfil, successfully, such a demanding role. Interviewing active Primary Care Group members they identify a set of core skills common to leadership situations at PCG level in the NHS. They suggest details of a management development programme to build these skills in the participants.

Graeme Currie and Stephen Procter argue from a slightly different perspective, drawing upon the critical human resource management literature, they analyse the role of the middle manager within health care organisational structures in England. They examine the opportunities (and situational constraints) presented to leaders and managers in the NHS to both set and operationalise health policy decisions.

Effective and ineffective leadership action is also examined by Paula Palmer, within the NHS in Wales. She considers the full range of leadership behaviours observable and analyses the effect of the different styles on the followers. Transformational leadership in fostering vision and encouraging trust and commitment is identified as the single most effective leadership style within the contexts examined. Gender as a leadership issue is also identified, followers preferring to be led by male leaders. The implications of this are explored.

Exploring and also proffering transformational style leadership, Mansour Jumaa and Jo Alleyne in their paper construct a leadership model for training potential clinical leaders within health care settings in transformational behaviours. The basis of their argument is that their model provides a framework for an evidence-based model of health care leadership training.

Leadership training and its effectiveness is a theme considered again in the paper by Zillyham Rojas, Dave Haran and Neil Marr. Training in health care management is evaluated in five developing countries in South America to assess the impact of the training programme on the enhancement of service delivery. Conclusions drawn are pessimistic regarding the effectiveness (in terms of hard measurable outcomes) of aid money spent in this way. However, the paper critiques its own approach (and those of others like it), in attempting to measure in a quick, simple and direct way what are complex and long-term development challenges intermixed with cultural issues.

Future Trends in Development

The last section in this collection considers possible future developments in the areas of OD as applied to health settings. More than this, it opens and widens a space to view alternative organising frameworks for the management, delivery and execution of health care services. It encourages us to 'think out of the box' to other possibilities.

The paper by Leonard Lerer and John Kimberley examines the health care sector from a European perspective. Based in France, they speculate as to the future of health care provision in a more closer linked, deregulated, European market for health provision, characterised by increasing consumer choice against the background of changing economic, social and demographic trends in the member states of the EU.

The paper by Steven Simeons and Robert McMaster returns the train of thought to the UK and to the NHS in particular. They initially take a historical perspective on the changing value system in the NHS as brought about by the introduction of the 'internal market' system. They argue that the competition engendered by this reform damaged the NHS family and its unitarist culture (perhaps irrevocably), moving working relationships between NHS stake-holders from one of 'trust' to an attitude now more likely to be characterised by calculative self-interest.

Donald Coid and Iain Crombie widen the debate beyond the NHS again, looking at the voluntary sector's contribution to health care provision within Scotland. They examine the evidence indicating levels of funding made to health voluntary organisations from the NHS in Scotland. They reveal dramatic regional differences in funding made available to voluntary organisations. They argue strongly that this limits the potential contribution able to be made by the voluntary sector in Scotland to carry out health care work easing the burden on the provision which has to be made by the statutory health agencies.

The final paper in this collection, looks at the growth in what it terms 'telehealth' that is to say, health care services delivered via the means of new technology. Sharon Levy and his colleagues in Dundee argue that the potential to access health care information via ones own efforts in the use of new technology could mark a considerable shift in the 'power' inherent in most health care relationships. Instead of expertise residing with the health professional telling and guiding patients in their treatment, telehealth could mean patients are able to become active, autonomous and empowered in searching out and responding to information that they now have access to. Whether this will mean that the relationship between patient and professional will become far less asymmetrical and much more democratic than at any other time in the past, is debated.

Concluding remarks

Health care provision is a service, a service does not exist without the people who deliver it and those who receive it. Exactly how best to organise, structure and facilitate that process such that the meeting of care providers with care receivers happens in the *most effective way possible* will remain an issue of considerable debate for as long as the service remains to be delivered. It is an issue that is constantly open and privy to the strong and legislative intervention of successive governments sometimes with and sometimes without the 'blessing' of the health care professionals themselves. We have learnt much over the past two decades about the effect of altering the nature of health care organisations and the way they function to deliver health care services. We must continue to examine, analyse and report findings on the on-going change in the organisation of health care to provide evidence upon which to base sound future decisions about the changes necessary to health care and its management.

We hope that you enjoy these contributions to the debate, and we look forward to welcoming you to SIHCM 2002 – to be held in St Andrews in spring of 2002.

Rosemary Rushmer, Huw Davies, Manouche Tavakoli, Mo Malek
Department of Management
University of St Andrews

*   For further information on SIHCM 2002 please email SIHCM@st-and.ac.uk

SECTION ONE
INVOLVEMENT AND
PARTNERSHIP
ARRANGEMENTS

Chapter One

Primary Care Groups – What are They and Why are They Here?

Lawrence Benson and Gillian Wright

Understanding PCGs

This chapter reports a study which explores factors affecting (inhibiting or promoting) the development of corporate board teams within complex and hybrid public sector organisations through a period of continuous transformation. The study takes executive board members for English PCGs as its unit of analysis for the period 1999 to 2002. This chapter explores the ways PCGs see their structure and objectives. It reviews the process of the formation of PCGs and presents an agenda arising from their nature which makes them a particularly interesting focus of research. The chapter summarises relevant literature, describes the research methods to be employed in the programme and presents results from the first phase of the study.

Establishing PCGs

The UK's National Health Service (NHS) is in a period of major reorganisation and probably this is no more radically felt than within the primary care sector. The current strategic direction for this attempt at health care reform can be found in the government White Paper *The New NHS, Modern and Dependable* (Department of Health (DoH), 1997) which addresses the NHS in England and this has heavily influenced health policy reform in other parts of the UK for example Scotland (Scottish Office DoH, 1997).

The purpose and role of PCGs in England and the NHS was announced in the government White Paper for England as bringing together:

Organisation Development in Health Care: Strategic Issues in Health Care Management, R.K. Rushmer, H.T.O. Davies, M. Tavakoli and M. Malek (eds), Ashgate Publishing Ltd, 2002.

Primary Care Groups comprising all GPs in an area together with community nurses will take responsibility for commissioning services for the local community. They will work closely with social services. There will be four options for the form that Primary Care Groups can take ... including the opportunity to become freestanding Primary Care Trusts, with responsibility for running community hospitals and community health services (DoH, 1997).

There are four levels of PCG outlined by government (ibid.) although PCGs were only initially established from April 1999 at levels 1 or 2.

Table 1.1   Four levels of PCG

Level	Status	Role	PCG/PCT
Level 1 from April 1999	Advisory subcommittee to the local Health Authority	Advice on commissioning health services for resident population	PCG
Level 2 from April 1999	Subcommittee to the local Health Authority with devolved responsibility	Commissioning some health services for resident population	PCG
Level 3 from April 2000	Freestanding public body – nationally accountable to the Secretary of State, locally accountable to the local health authority	Commissioning some health services for resident population	PCG and PCT
Level 4 from April 2000	Freestanding public body – nationally accountable to the Secretary of State, locally accountable to the local health authority	Commissioning health services and providing some community health services for resident population	PCG and PCT

PCGs are thus seen by government as a major initiative to formally institutionalise collaboration and partnership. This trend of being formally required to work in partnership is now evident across UK health and social care (DoH, 1997, 1998). Thus the effectiveness of institutionalised collaboration has become a major focus of practice and research within UK public sector management.

PCGs are of interest as a research focus for a number of reasons as noted in Table 1.2.

Table 1.2   PCGs as a research focus

Newness	The invited debate about their newness of approach (Maynard, 1998)
Scale	The national scale of the policy initiative; all England to be covered by PCGs from April
Roles	The declared breadth of the role of PCGs encompassing potentially both provision and commission of health services
Formality	PCGs as an initiative which formally institutionalises collaboration and partnership in government
Membership	The wide membership of their executive boards and the consequent mix of organisational cultural back grounds
Transitional period	The period of transition of shadow and live PCGs (including PCTs) from 1998 to at least 2002

The Nature of PCGs

The details of PCGs noted in Table 1.3 demonstrate the variety in their size/ scale. Overall, the government intention of PCGs serving 100,000 local residents has been largely realised from April 1999. The level of complexity within most PCGs is made apparent by the large number of GP practices working within their boundaries. There is also some evidence of an apparent inequality regarding the availability of resources targeted for the management and organisational infrastructure of PCGs.

Membership of PCG Boards

PCG boards for levels 1 and 2 are multi-professional, GP-dominated, tied with existing organisational structures (subcommittees of the Health Authority) and have new categories of membership from outside health structures, e.g. social service and lay representation.

In respect to the board membership at levels 1 and 2 this consists of:

- four to seven general practitioners;
- one to two nurses working within the community;
- one local authority social services officer;
- one lay member to represent local people;
- one health authority non-executive director;
- one chief executive officer (ex-officio membership);
- the overwhelming majority of PCGs are chaired by a GP.

Table 1.3   The nature of PCGs – April 1999 to October 2000

Population served

Government envisaged size of PCGs	100,000 residents
Average size of population served by a PCG from April 1999	107,000 residents
Minimum size of population served by a PCG from April 1999	47,000 residents
Maximum size of population served by a PCG from April 1999	278,000 residents

Number of GP practices served

Average number of GP practices within a PCG	19
Minimum number of GP practices within a PCG	5
Maximum number of GP practices within a PCG	66

Financial allocations

Average size of PCG financial allocation	£43.6 million
Smallest PCG financial allocation	£1.5 million
Largest PCG financial allocation	£127 million
Smallest management budget for a PCG	£119,000
Largest management budget for a PCG	£1.28 million
The PCG population and its four levels	
PCGs established in April 1999	481
PCGs from April 1999 at Level 1	82 (17% of PCG total)
PCGs from April 1999 at Level 2	399 (83% of PCG total)
PCGs who will become PCTs in April 2000	17
PCGs who will become PCTs in October 2000	40 approximately

Sources: DoH (1997), Audit Commission (1999 and 2000) and Kent and Kumar (1999).

It was not until the passage of the Health Act 1999 that legislation was in place for PCGs to pursue the more radical levels of 3 and 4 which give Primary Care Trust (PCT) status. There will be 17 PCTs in England from April 2000 and more to follow in October 2000. The membership for PCTs (PCG levels 3 and 4) is different to that of PCGs levels 1 and 2. There have been comparisons made between level 4 PCTs and US Health Maintenance Organisations (HMOs), which both have the hybrid role of providing and commissioning services (Devlin and Smith, 1999).

Understanding Collaborative Organisations – the Literature

There is an established conceptual base in the literature, which provides frameworks to analyse the formulation, development and impact of such collaborative organisations (Schon, 1971; Gray, 1989; Kanter, 1994; Hudson, 1999; Meads, 1999; Pratt et al., 1999). This conceptual base can be linked to a range of general literature domains, for example leadership, effective teams (Hackman, 1990; Katzenbach and Smith, 1993), organisational design with reference to hybrid organisations (Mintzberg, 1983), public sector management (Hood, 1991; Ferlie et al., 1996), systems theory (Checkland, 1990) and, particularly, whole systems theory (Morgan, 1997; Pratt et al., 1998).

Also of relevance here is the literature surrounding health policy within primary care and, specifically, the effectiveness of the primary health care team (West and Slater, 1996; Poulton and West, 1997) and primary care purchasing (Le Grand et al., 1998), the latter predating the advent of PCGs.

The main issues from this literature are the recognition of hybrid organisational forms and the awareness that these hybrid forms are under-researched, especially in the UK health sector. This literature review also highlights that multi-agency alliances need for facilitative leadership.

Evaluating the Existing PCG Literature

PCGs are a recent policy initiative and so limited research is available. Research already undertaken includes literature reviews, surveys, case studies and multi-method studies and there is also a considerable range of commentary by practitioners and academics. Table 1.4 summarises these studies and categorises them according to their macro (i.e. national, e.g. Marks and Hunter, 1998), meso (i.e. Health Authority, e.g. Regen et al., 1999) or micro focus (i.e. within the PCG, e.g. Wilson et al., 1998).

Research Method

The research programme is a longitudinal study spanning April 1999 to April 2002.

Phase 1	Establishing teams – 1999
Phase 2	Managing teams in transition – 2000
Phase 3	Understanding team development – 2000
Phases 4 and 5	Effectiveness of PCGs / PCTs – 2001/2002.

Phase 1: Establishing Teams – Summer 1999

The first phase of the programme is now complete, i.e. a preliminary study based primarily in West Yorkshire (within the NHS Northern and Yorkshire regional area) which took place in the summer of 1999.

Table 1.4   Analysis of PCG emergent literature 1998 to February 2000

Style of source/research method	Macro – at the wider health care system level	Meso – at the local health authority level	Micro – at the PCG level and sub PCG level e.g. the Primary Health Care Team, the integrated nursing team
Comment - practitioner	Chisholm (1998)		Christie and Blades (1998)
Comment – academic	Maynard (1998) Klein (1998) Chambers and Lucking (1998) Cook (1998) Mays and Goodwin (1998)	Pratt et al. (1998) Hudson (1999)	Parkin (1999a, b and c)
Meta review	Le Grand et al. (1998)		
Literature review	Lewis (1999)	Wilson (1998)	
Archival – secondary research	Audit Commission (1999)		West and Slater (1996)
Survey	Bruce and Forbes (1999)	Kent and Kumar (1999)	Poulton and West (1997) Malbon, and Mays (1998)
Case study	Hunter, Marks and Sykes (2000)		Macleod et al. (1999)
Delphi			Wilson et al. (1998b)
Qualitative	Marks and Hunter (1998)		Benson and Wright (1999)
Mixed methods	Audit Commission (2000)	Regen et al. (1999) Shapiro (99) Meads (1999)	Smith et al. (1999)

Phase 1 was designed to offer a means of exploring the initial perceptions and expectations from PCG board members of their roles and that of PCGs. The objectives of this phase of the study included:

1   exploring different perceptions of the PCG role;
2   exploring the PCG board as a new team with specific reference to team inputs, processes and outputs gained through the use of an established theoretical framework which has been designed to examine effective teams within primary health care (West and Slater, 1996; Poulton and West, 1997);
3   gaining an insight to the specific role of the community nurse as a PCG board member;
4   gaining an insight to the concept of partnership within the context of the PCG board when working with local agencies. This objective was addressed by:

   a) application of an established conceptual framework for partnership between health and social care organisations (Pratt et al., 1998); and
   b) identification of the factors that either inhibited or progressed partnership across its four levels of partnership within the PCG context;

5   exploring the concept of a hybrid organisation with board members.

The initial findings of the study were presented to the September 1999 Public Administration Committee Conference, which can be viewed on line (Benson and Wright, 1999). The intention of this chapter is not to represent these initial findings but to give a second analysis of the data. This concentrates on perceptions of the role of PCG (objective 1), partnership (particularly objective 4b) and hybrid organisations (objective 5).

Phase 2: Managing Teams in Transition – June to November 2000

A national postal survey is to be administered through a self-completed questionnaire. This will be distributed in June to August 2000 and analysed in Autumn 2000.

The objective of this phase of the study will be to establish an overview of issues related to the development of teams in transition and expected partnership across a national sample of PCG board members.

The sampling frame for this phase of the study will be the listing of PCGs and their board members held by the NHS Executive. The sample to be taken from the whole population of English PCGs will be stratified, based upon the four PCG levels (by this point within the study there should be 17 PCTs and another 40+ PCGs ready to become PCTs in October 2000).

The identifiable strata existing within the overall population of PCGs (currently 481 PCGs) by summer 2000 will be:

- PCGs which have been confirmed as PCTs in April 2000 – estimated at 17 or 3.5 per cent of the PCG population;
- PCGs aiming to start as PCTs in October 2000 – estimated at 40 or 8.5 per cent of the PCG population;
- PCGs to remain at PCG level 1 throughout the financial year 2000/01 – estimated at 81 or 17 per cent of the population;
- PCGs to remain at PCG level 2 throughout the financial year 2000/01 – estimated at 342 or 71 per cent of the original population.

Although the senior structures between PCGs levels 1 and 2 and PCTs (PCG levels 3 and 4) differ, all PCGs have an executive group where there is a mix of health professionals (which at the executive board of levels 1 and 2 and the executive team of levels 3 and 4 have large GP representation), social care and managerial representatives. Therefore a chair, chief executive, GP, community nurse and social services representative will be selected from each of the sampled PCGs as recipients for questionnaires.

The sampling exercise for the postal survey would have to take account of the possible examples in PCT applications for mergers between existing PCGs. This will alter the size of each of the four strata of PCGs. Analysis from the survey will be targeted for dissemination in a peer reviewed journal for early 2001.

Phase 3: Understanding Team Development – July to December 2000

During summer and autumn 2000 there will be a second series of in-depth interviews of PCG board members drawn from the Northern and Yorkshire regional area.

The objectives of this phase of the study will be to identify challenges in team development and to look for resolution strategies when creating hybrid organisations.

Four PCGs will be selected, one from each of the four strata identified above. The range of interviewees would reflect the mix of professional and organisational backgrounds on a PCG executive board and from each PCG it is hoped to at least interview one person from the same categories again, as with the postal survey of chair, chief executive officer, GP, community nurse and social services representative. It is hoped that these interviews will be repeated twice for the remaining two years of the study in phases 4 and 5.

Phases 4 and 5: Effectiveness of PCGs/PCTs 2001/2002

The objectives of this phase of the study will be to review initial outputs from PCGs/PCTs.

A second national survey of PCGs will be held in Autumn 2001, again to be targeted at the people represented in the first survey.

The use of two principal data collection methods (i.e. postal questionnaire survey and face to face interviews) is deliberate to enable data and methodological triangulation (Bryman, 1988; Easterby-Smith et al., 1991).

Research Method of Phase 1 – Summer 1999

The data collection method for this phase comprised 13 semi-structured interviews with board members of PCGs and Health Authority staff involved in the development of PCGs. Semi-structured interviewing was seen as appropriate to give some flexibility to pursue emerging issues (Frankfort-Nachmias and Nachmias, 1996). The interviews were held in May and June 1999. Interviewees who were PCG board members had only been working in this role since Autumn 1998 (when PCG boards where in 'shadow' form) with only two to three months experience following the launch of PCGs in April 1999.

Nine out of the 13 interviews were held with people working within or associated with five PCGs within the Bradford and Calderdale boundaries and a further three people from three Health Authority areas also involved in PCG development. The selection of individual interviewees was to have at least one person from each type of PCG board member.

PCG board members:

> one lay representative;
> three nurse members;
> two chief executive officers;
> one general practitioner;
> one chair and general practitioner;
> one social services representative;
> one Health Authority non-executive director representative.

Other interviewees:

> two Health Authority–organisational development managers;
> one Health Authority primary care nurse adviser.

Results from Phase 1

The output from the interviews which relates to PCG roles, hybrid forms and partnerships are presented in this section. It is the issue of partnership which stimulated most comment as a radical and challenging concept that respondents were having to address.

(a) PCGs' Role

There were some differences in emphasis from interviewees regarding the newness of the fundamental role of PCGs. However, most interviewees believed that there was a new role and aim of PCGs.

> I think that the [PCG] board accepts that the remit of the PCG goes much beyond the traditional NHS health care. The focus is much more on a more coordinated approach to improving health and therefore it is essential, it is a prerequisite that you as a group, as an organisation, need to work with the other agencies that are impacting on whatever objectives you set within that framework (Chief Executive).

Many noted, however, that the recent local history of primary care commissioning was undeniably influential (whether this be GP commissioning, GP fundholding or total purchasing) in shaping PCGs.

One interviewee saw that the role of PCGs could potentially be quite destructive and undermine the freedom of GPs and undo the positive work completed by GP fundholders:

> We had a very good framework under fund holding which was commissioning across a large chunk of population, about 60,000 patients. So we had a very good system and we were trying to develop new patterns of care delivery along with other providers (GP).

However most interviewees saw PCGs as an evolution from different forms of primary care commissioning and were extremely positive about the future for PCGs as new board members.

(b)   Hybrid Forms

It was recognised that one of the challenges posed by PCGs was to try and work with people and organisations with very different cultures and structures and the idea of PGCs as a hybrid organisation was discussed with some interviewees. One interviewee noted that the intention of PCT trust status was to reshape health and social care organisations into a new type of hybrid, but how to get to this position of an effective hybrid was at that time unclear:

> PCTs will start to then bring in other organisations, and we might see a movement of the boundaries between the various public sector organisations. We might see that the split is no longer health service, social services, whatever, but they will become rather different shaped organisations (Health Authority non-executive director).

(c)   *Wider Partnership between Public Sector Organisations*

There was a difference in opinions regarding the newness of PCGs as a formal mechanism for partnership between local agencies. Ranging from one PCG Chief Executive who rejected that PCGs were not totally new but an extension of the GP commissioning within the area interviewees who saw this as a different and new opportunity to develop partnership across agencies.

Throughout the interviews four levels of partnership were identified. These comprised partnership between:

- PCG board members;
- PCG board members and the colleagues they represent outside the board;
- PCGs; and
- the PCG and other agencies not directly represented on the board.

This acted as a useful framework with which to summarise the factors named by interviewees that either inhibited or encouraged partnership.

Inhibitors to Partnership

(i) Partnership between the PCG board members:

- the lack of time available for board members to perform their roles;
- the lack of clarity of others' roles. Some resistance to the wider membership

and fuller equality of membership on a PCG board than had happened in previous primary care purchasing initiatives, this was clearly evident from the interview with the GP board member:

> The reality is that primary care has been financed, rightly or wrongly, via general practitioners and the organisation, rightly or wrongly, is being set up by general practitioners because we're small businesses and our livelihood depends on it, and we are acutely aware therefore when it comes to paying your mortgage with your month end cheque of changes that are forced on us. So for other people to say, 'We need to have an equal voice', is all very well but who's paying the mortgage on the building that they're having an equal voice in?;

• the variety of organisational cultures represented by those on the board. This was highlighted in the interviews, a representative comment coming from one of the two Chief Executives interviewed:

> The biggest one is the cultures are so completely different, so if you think of the culture of the local authority, any local authority, it's different to the culture of the Health Service, and there's also thrown in the culture of primary care into those, which is different again to a NHS Trust culture, Health Authority culture, you know, it's very very different …;

• the variety of professional tribes and boundaries which are represented on the board

> Traditional professional protectiveness for example, health visiting, this idea that we have a monopoly on Primary Care … And I think we need to step down a bit and step back and realise that a lot of other agencies are interested in health … and have a lot to offer (nurse);

• different past and current funding streams and financial responsibilities between the agencies/organisations represented on the PCG board, e.g. NHS Trust (through community nurse members), social services, local health authority and GP practices.

(ii) Partnership between board members and the colleagues they represent outside the board but who work within the geographical boundaries of the PCG:

• lack of time to meet with other colleagues as well as meeting on the PCG board;
• lack of understanding of the board members role by colleagues within the PCG but outside the PCG board e.g. local nurses seeing the community

nurse board members as a trade union representative rather than an executive board nurse;
- tensions between individual GP practices and the new PCG board – clash of the independent practitioner running essentially small business faced with unified budgets and the larger PCG organisation.

(iii) Partnership between the PCG and other neighbouring PCGs:

- Some competition for resources in a bidding culture and ambitions to reach PCT status in an area.

(iv) Partnership with other agencies and organisations not represented on the board:

- lack of time and money to resource the delivery of care whilst involved in PCG business to meet with other colleagues as well as on the PCG board;
- the scale and amount of change across all public services following the 1997 general election where new mechanisms for inter-agency partnership and collaboration have been established e.g. Health Action Zones (HAZs), Educational Action Zones, the Sure Start initiative for preschool children.

Encouraging Factors

(i) Partnership between the PCG board members:

- previously established working relationships of a core of people in most PCGs within the study;
- early successes based upon small projects;
- the richer mix of professional backgrounds and individual experience represented within a PCG board than had previously occurred in other forms of primary care commissioning.

(ii) Partnership between board members and the colleagues they represent outside the board but who work within the geographical boundaries of the PCG:

- setting up of structures that will feed directly into the PCG board e.g. forums for particular professional groups (nursing, practice managers, GPs), localities within the PCG boundaries, and specific project groups.

(iii) Partnership between the PCG and other neighbouring PCGs:

- common structures across the local health authority areas e.g. the Health Improvement Programme (HiMP) the HAZ and mini HAZs based on PCG boundaries. Existing and new professional groups drawn from the individual PCGs but meeting together to discuss common professional issues, e.g. nurses, practice managers.

(iv) Partnership with other agencies and organisations not represented on the board:

- a history of joint services of planning across agencies.

At least one interviewee (one of the nurse members from a health visiting background) was becoming personally involved in a parallel partnership exercise to PCGs. This was based on the 'Sure Start' model of improving service provision for the under-3s within the context of social exclusion.

Conclusions

The conclusions from phase 1 of the study are:

- the role of PCGs has significant distinctions from its antecedents and is extremely challenging in scale, although PCGs were influenced by previous primary care commissioning initiatives;
- there was some recognition by some interviewees that PCTs would eventually represent new forms of hybrid organisation;
- there was a wide range of factors that were identified which could promote or inhibit partnership both within the PCG itself and outside the PCG within the complexities of the local health/social care system. Inhibiting factors included the lack of time and lack of clarity of PCG board member roles, the existence of professional tribes and different organisational cultural backgrounds of board members, some mourning for previous primary care commissioning initiatives, different past and existing financial systems, some competition between PCGs, geographical boundaries and in general the huge scale of change across the public sector in a locality;
- drivers for change were identified as established working relationships between board members, the success of early small scale projects, the rich

mix of different professional and organisational backgrounds, the creation of infrastructure within the boundaries of the PCG to involve more professional groups, common partnership and collaborative infrastructure across a local area and across PCGs with other local agencies.

Discussion/Implications

It was clear from the study that four types of partnership lead to different challenges and combining this outcome with the well established model of team effectiveness (Poulton and West, 1997) a framework for analysis emerges to further study the diagnosis of PCG establishment, management and effectiveness. This is represented in systems form in Figure 1.1.

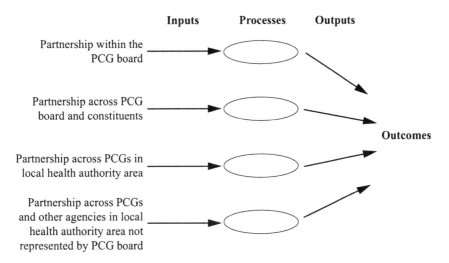

Figure 1.1 Primary care groups as examples of partnership system

Acknowledgements

Thanks to all those interviewed in the preliminary study for this chapter from Airedale, Bradford City, Bradford South and West, Calderdale PCGs, Kirklees and East London and the City Health Authorities.

References

Audit Commission (1999), *PCGs an Early View of Primary Care Groups in England*, Belmont Press, Northampton.

Audit Commission (2000), *The PCG Agenda – Early Progress of Primary Care Groups in the 'New NHS'*, Audit Commission, London.

Benson, L. and Wright, G. (1999), 'Exploring the Structure and Processes of Collaborative Local Health Care Commissioning with Particular Reference to One Professional Group within the New National Health Service Hybrid Organisational Form – Primary Care Groups (PCGs)', *Public Administration Committee, 29th Annual Conference September 1999*, Civil Service College, Sunningdale: http://www.york.ac.uk/depts/poli/pac/papers/benson.htm.

Bruce, A. and Forbes, T. (1999), 'Co-operation and Collaboration in the Delivery of Health Care:Implementing Change in Scotland', *Public Administration Committee, 29th Annual Conference September 1999*, Civil Service College, Sunningdale: http://www.york.ac.uk/depts/poli/pac/papers/benson.htm.

Bryman, A. (1988), *Quantity and Quality in Social Research*, London, Routledge.

Chambers, R. and Lucking, A. (1998), 'Partners in Time? Can PCGs Really Succeed where Others have Failed?', *British Journal of Health Care Management*, 4 (10), pp. 489–91.

Checkland, P. and Scholes, J. (1990), *Soft Systems Methodology in Action*, John Wiley and Sons, Chichester.

Chisholm, J. (1998), 'Primary Care and the NHS White Papers', *British Medical Journal*, 316 (7146), pp. 1687–8.

Christie, S. and Blades, S. (1998), 'Toil and Trouble', *Health Service Journal*, 108 (5603), pp. 30–31.

Cook, T. (1998), 'New Labour, New NHS … New Internal Market', *Management Accounting*, 76 (3), pp. 24–6.

Department of Health (1997), *The New NHS, Modern and Dependable*, Cmd 3807, The Stationery Office, London.

Department of Health (1998), *Modernising Social Services – Promoting Independence, Improving Protection, Raising Standards*, The Stationery Office, London.

Devlin, M. and Smith, J. (1999), 'States of Flux', *Health Service Journal*, Vol. 109, (5563), 6 May, pp. 24–5.

Easterby-Smith, M., Thorpe, R. and Lowe, A. (1991), *Management Research – an Introduction*, Sage, London.

Ferlie, E., Pettigrew, A., Ashburner, L. and Fitzgerald, L. (1996), *The New Public Management in Action*, Oxford University Press, Oxford.

Frankfort-Nachmias, C. and Nachmias, D. (1996), *Research Methods in the Social Sciences*, 5th edn, Edward Arnold, London.

Gray, B. (1989), 'Collaboration – The Constructive Management of Differences from Collaboration: Finding common ground for Multiparty Problems', in G. Robinson Hickman (ed.), *Leading Organizations: Perspectives for a New Era*, Sage, London.

Hackman, J.R. (ed.) (1990), *Groups that Work (and Those that Don't):Creating conditions for effective teamwork*, Jossey Bass, San Francisco.

Hood, C. (1991), 'A Public Management for all Seasons?', *Public Administration*, 69 (Spring), pp. 3–19.

Hudson, B. (1999), 'Joint Commissioning across the Primary Health Care–Social Care Boundary: Can it work?', *Health and Social Care in the Community*, 7 (5), pp. 358–66.

Kanter, R.M. (1994), 'Collaborative Advantage: The art of alliances', *Harvard Business Review*, 72 (4), pp. 96–108.

Katzenbach, J.R. and Smith, D.K. (1993),*The Wisdom of Teams – Creating High Performance Organization*, Harvard Business Press, Boston.

Kent, A. and Kumar, A. (1999), *The Development Needs of Primary Care Groups*, PCG NHS Alliance, Chichester.

Klein, R. (1998), 'Why Britain is Reorganizing its National Health Service – Yet Again', *Health Affairs*, 17 (4), pp. 111–25.

Le Grand, J., Mays, N. and Mulligan, J. (eds) (1998), *Learning from the Internal Market – a Review of the Evidence*, King's Fund, London.

Lewis, J. (1999), 'The Concepts of Community Care and Primary Care in the UK: The 1960s to the 1990s', *Health and Social Care in the Community*, 7 (5), pp. 333–41.

Marks, L. and Hunter, D.J. (1998), *The Development of Primary Care Groups: Policy into practice*, The NHS Confederation, Birmingham.

Mays, N. and Goodwin, N. (1998), 'Primary Care Groups in England' in R. Klein (ed.), *Implementing the White Paper – Pitfalls and Opportunities*, King's Fund, London.

Maynard, A. (1998), 'GP Fund Holding is Dead!: Long live the new primary care groups', *British Journal of Health Care Management*, 4 (10), pp. 469–71.

Meads, G. (1999), 'Research Matrix Reveals Typology of Primary Care Groups', *British Journal of Health Care Management*, 5 (3), pp. 96–100.

Mintzberg, H. (1983), *Structure in Fives – Designing Effective Organizations*, Prentice Hall, London.

Morgan, G. (1997), *Images of Organizations*, 2nd edn, Sage, London.

Parkin, P. (1999a), 'Managing Change in the Community 1: The case of PCGs', *British Journal of Community Nursing*, 4 (1), pp. 19–27.

Parkin, P. (1999b), Managing Change in the Community 2: Partnership in PCGs', *British Journal of Community Nursing*, 4 (4), pp. 188–95.

Parkin, P. (1999c), Managing Change in the Community 3: Conflict in PCGs', *British Journal of Community Nursing*, 4 (6), pp. 275–82.

Poulton, B. and West, M. (1997), 'Defining and Measuring Effectiveness for Primary Health Care Teams', in P. Pearson and J. Spencer (eds), *Promoting Teamwork in Primary Care*, Arnold, London.

Pratt, J., Plamping, D. and Gordon, P. (1998), *Partnership: Fit for Purpose? – Whole Systems Thinking – Working Paper Series*, King's Fund, London.

Pratt, J., Gordon, P. and Plamping, D. (1999), *Working Whole Systems: Putting theory into practice in organisations*, King's Fund, London.

Regen, E., Smith, J. and Shapiro, J. (1999), *First Off the Starting Block: Lessons from GP commissioning pilots for Primary Care Groups*, Health Services Management Centre – University of Birmingham, Birmingham.

Shapiro, J. (1999), 'The First Six Months of PCGS', in *Primary Care Group NHS Alliance, 8 to 9 September 1999, 2nd Annual Conference*, unpublished, Birmingham.

Schon, D. (1971), *Beyond the Stable State: Public and private learning in a changing society*, Maurice Temple Smith, London.

Smith, K., Dickson, M. and Sheaff, R. (1999), 'Second among Equals', *Nursing Times*, 95 (13), 31 March, pp. 54–5.

The Scottish Office Department of Health (1997), *Designed to Care Renewing the National Health Service in Scotland*, Cmd 3811, The Stationery Office, Edinburgh.

West, M.A. and Slater, J. (1996), *Teamworking in Primary Health Care: A review of its effectiveness*, Health Education Authority, London.

Wilson, T. (1998), *Primary Care Group Development: Lessons from the literature*, Primary Care Group Resource Unit, Oxford: http://strauss.ihs.ox.ac.uk/pcgru/development.html.

Wilson, T., Butler, F. and Watson, M. (1998), *Defining the Education and Training Needs of Primary Care Groups – A Report from a two part Delphi consultation and Consensus Conference*, PCG Resource Unit, Oxford.

Chapter Two

Setting up Local Health Groups in Wales: Challenges and Opportunities

Stephanie Williams

Introduction

Local Health Groups went live in Wales on 1 April 1999. Nearly one year on, it is appropriate to ask how the LHGs are progressing. The chapter will argue that although the new structural arrangements are in line with current organisational thinking about decentralised decision-making (Harrison et al., 1992), the implementation process has been problematic. The chapter examines the opportunities and challenges facing these fledgling organisations as they set about four key tasks:

1   developing the multi-disciplinary Board of 18 members into a cohesive team;
2   setting priorities for the LHG;
3   creating a corporate identity;
4   developing working relationships with stakeholder agencies.

The chapter first describes the policy and organisational contexts within which Local Health Groups have been established. It is based on the findings of two studies. Survey 1's findings illustrate the range of problems likely to be faced by the new organisations. Results from the second survey describe the challenges and opportunities LHG Chairmen perceived themselves facing in their first nine months of activity.

The second survey focused on Local Health Group chairmen as key players in setting up these new organisations. The chairmen's views of the opportunities and constraints facing them have been chosen as a means of highlighting the dilemmas for those involved in developing primary care. The findings are

Organisation Development in Health Care: Strategic Issues in Health Care Management, R.K. Rushmer, H.T.O. Davies, M. Tavakoli and M. Malek (eds), Ashgate Publishing Ltd, 2002.

based on face-to-face interviews with each of the 22 LHG chairmen between July and December 1999. The chapter concludes with recommendations for further organisational development activity to help LHGs perform their new roles effectively to begin to meet the challenge of improving the health of their local populations.

Context

Government Policy Context

This study took place against a background of a major shift in government policy for the NHS over the past decade. *Working for Patients* (Department of Health, 1989) aimed to encourage quality, choice, and access through diversified local services. The current policy drive aims to capture some of the benefits realised by that shift, and to effect further movement away from the individual patient perspective to the local population's needs (Department of Health: NHS Wales, 1998). Uniformity of quality and equity of access brought about through collaborative partnerships are the order of the day. These new primary care structures, as decentralised local units, free to develop creative responses to local needs, within clearly defined strategic goals and performance monitoring frameworks (Harrison et al., 1992), may well be fitting vehicles to implement this policy effectively.

The 'Welsh Dimension'

The National Assembly is bringing a new dimension to the development of health policy in Wales. Although it is too soon to draw firm conclusions about the impact of the new Assembly, it is already clear that it is bringing a new energy and an element of democracy to this process. Clear accountability frameworks between the Assembly and Trust and Health Authority Chairmen and Chief Officers have been created. At the same time a new corporacy is emerging within NHS Wales, with a strengthening of central leadership (NHS Wales, 1999).

Local Organisational Context

To deliver these policy intentions, Local Health Groups have been created in Wales (Department of Health, 1998) with different incentives than those available to English practices, forming into primary care organisations. Key differences are:

- *development potential*: PCOs have four levels of development culminating in autonomous bodies, with the option to become fully fledged independent bodies (Primary Care Trusts). This option is not currently available to LHGs;
- *coterminosity*: LHGs have been set up to be coterminous to local authority boundaries. To further facilitate intersectoral collaboration, two local authority representatives are integral members of the LHG Board, one of whom is normally a social services representative;
- *size*: the LHG Boards consist of 18 members (not 12 as in the English model); this includes scope for two members to represent the public, one drawn from the voluntary sector (NHS Wales 1998);
- *responsible officers*: in the Welsh model the responsible officer is entitled 'General Manager' compared to the 'Chief Executive' responsible for the PCOs. Furthermore the GM is a Health Authority employee, and carries a formal and substantive Health Authority portfolio (e.g. Director of Finance) alongside their LHG roles.

Additionally, the financial incentives to form LHGs are rather more subtle than those previously on offer to fundholders, where individual GPs and partnerships were able to reinvest any savings they made from changes in referral or prescribing patterns *within their own practices.*

Furthermore, significant changes were taking place among other key stakeholder agencies in Wales during the period preceding the establishment of LHGs. Health Authorities reduced from 12 to five in 1997. Between 1 April and end December 1999, the first nine months of LHG life, major changes at senior level occurred within four of the five Welsh Health Authorities: in one, three different Chief Executives were in post during this period. These changes may have adversely affected the support and direction available to LHGs.

The reconfiguration of Trusts, down from 29 to 16 within Wales within the preceding year, may also have had an impact on the establishment of LHGs. Senior Trust managers faced displacement which was not conducive to an outward or developmental focus, although Trusts now have a new statutory duty to consult with their LHG Boards about service developments locally.

The Local Context: Results of the Telephone/Email Survey

The first survey showed that many GPs are reluctant collaborators with LHGs rather than active proponents. Complaints about the 'political' nature of those elected as LHG Chair and Board members were frequently voiced. Fund-holders expressed real anger at what they perceived as whole-scale destruction of the improvements they had wrought.

The survey indicated that specific challenges facing Chairmen as LHGs went live on 1 April included a pervading pessimism among the local GP community arising from:

- uncertainty due to a perceived paucity of information and lack of direction;
- perception that standards of care prevailing locally would inevitably fall to the lowest common denominator
- fear of control from the centre, particularly in relation to the clinical governance agenda; this was expressed along three dimensions:
  - HA to LHG;
  - LHG to practice;
  - LHG to individual GP level;
- perceived inability to influence the LHG agenda;
- insufficient incentives: financial and professional;
- perception of LHG as scapegoat for decisions which should be taken elsewhere, e.g. as a rationing device.

However, against this challenging background at national level, LHGs can be viewed as a positive step towards improving the population focus within primary care and a genuinely revolutionary attempt to bring about local decision-making in search of 'seamless care', in a context traditionally fraught with interagency suspicion and competition.

The second survey illustrates the ways in which chairmen have faced these challenges.

Progress to Date: Preliminary Results Based on Initial Analysis of Baseline Interviews with LHG Chairmen: August to December 1999

Chairmen's Roles

All but three of the 22 chairmen are GPs, in line with guidance issued (NHS

Wales, 1998). All are males, mostly in the 45+ age group; two are pharmacists, and one is a Director of Social Services; three are recently retired.

Without exception, the chairmen expressed a deep personal commitment to 'make a difference' to primary care development as their prime motivating force in taking up the role of chairman. The chairmen's focus, the way they see their roles and who they include in their definition of their constituents varies markedly across the 22 LHGs. Few describe themselves as thinking strategically at this stage; the majority are more operationally oriented. This may reflect the pressing need to set up their organisations from scratch.

Figure 2.1 indicates a predominating focus on the professional community as opposed to the wider local community. Since one of the main thrusts behind establishing LHGs was to 'improve the health of the local population' this professional orientation may prove problematic (NHS Wales, 1998).

	Inclusive	Exclusive
Strategic	4	5
Operational	5	8

Key

Inclusive: denotes definition of constituents which encompasses local community.
Exclusive: restricts definition of constituents to local GPs and/or professional community.
Strategic: focuses on remit of improving local population's health.
Operational: focuses on more specific local developments.

Figure 2.1   LHG chairmen's focus

Chairmen's Training and Development

Training for newly-appointed chairmen was provided centrally, under the auspices of the Postgraduate School within the University of Wales College of Medicine, by the NHS Staff College Wales and the Institute for Medical and Social Care Applied Research, University of Wales Bangor, in the form of three two-day modules between January and July 1999. The training aimed to scope the parameters of the roles the LHGs would need to perform and included sessions on Clinical Governance, Commissioning, Finance etc. This broad brush, topic-based approach was supplemented by formation of a peer group support network. The chairmen were then responsible, alongside their HA colleagues, for arranging appropriate board-level development activities.

Setting up the New Organisations

Not unexpectedly, the setting-up phase dominated the first nine months of LHG life.

Corporate premises The extent to which these fledgling organisations have been able to establish their own identities may well be dependent on whether or not they have their own corporate premises. Two of the 22 had no premises at all at the end of December, eight months after going live, and a full year since first being formed in shadow mode. This may have had an adverse impact on an LHG's ability to form a cohesive team of its board and secretariat. Most moved straight into the newly vacated quarters of the former Commissioning Teams, again giving a clear message from the Health Authority as to its perception of the status of the LHG. Several have their offices within the Health Authority's headquarters. One was denied permission to move to premises within a Local Authority-owned building, while two others from different HAs have successfully done so. It remains to be demonstrated whether this physical proximity facilitates closer cross-sectoral working relationships in practice.

Secretariat appointments In October several were still struggling to finalise key appointments within their secretariats. The degree of real choice afforded to the new chairmen as they made these crucial appointments was constrained by the Health Authorities' needs to reduce their own staff numbers. The reality is that the general manager roles are Health Authority appointments and each holds a substantive HA portfolio.

   Thus, in this first year of activity, chairmen faced several hurdles inherent in the structure: potentially divided loyalties of their chief operating officers; HA constraints on their freedom of choice of secretariat appointees; and delays in getting premises and people into post. This need for chairmen to concentrate on operational tasks may well have been detrimental to the process of developing a corporate vision. For example, in coming to meet with each chairman, they were frequently to be found typing their own letters, working from their own surgeries and struggling to control papers across three sites: their own homes, surgeries and their LHG premises.

Developing a Corporate Identity

Most chairmen mentioned the new demands of corporacy they were experiencing and trying to transmit to their members:

> I think there are one or two people who really don't understand what they've let themselves in for, I think that's the message which I give to them. I think they don't appreciate the discipline of the corporate governance, they don't understand that they have been elected and selected to a publicly accountable body, and that they have to be very careful that they don't align themselves to groups which may cause conflict of interest ...

Another chairman spoke of his frustrations on this score: 'The independent contractors have a small business mentality that is trying, sometimes, personally, so there are real culture clashes ...'. This chairman went on to say however: 'I think there is a creative tension in disagreements and I can foster that. We need to build a new unique culture for the group.' Building this new culture is going to be a slow and difficult process. As Stephen Henry points out 'The quickest way to turn off the GP is to tell him he needs some teambuilding or management skills and that time is needed to develop mutual understanding, trust and ways of working together ...' (Henry, 1999, p. 16). In such circumstances, trying to identify some early successes is proving to be a popular strategy both in terms of the board itself and its wider constituents. Again this reflects an operational rather than strategic focus. Added constraints on the development of a corporate focus then have been the competing expectations and differing cultures of Health Authorities and LHGs, including the different languages each uses, as well as the lack of organisational capacity mentioned earlier.

Teambuilding among a Multi-disciplinary Board of 18

Most chairmen used some form of semi-social gathering to begin to form working relationships within their boards. Several were very conscious of the need to ensure that all members of the board were helped to feel that they had a contribution to make to the LHG's work. All chairmen were conscious of the need to ensure that the board was not overtly manipulated by any one professional group. Since in several cases the elected GPs (and some chairmen) were also LMC members, this was potentially difficult. As one GP chairman put it: 'You know, in one sense you're given a task as it were to do, and you have to go away and do it – but you're [also a] representative of your colleagues ....'

This same chairman elaborates:

> ... we have some dysfunction around the Group, because one of the doctors has insisted he wants a doctors' group, which I didn't think was appropriate and we've had some harsh words about it, and we've had to agree to disagree ...

The relationship between these new organisations (LHGs) and existing holders of the territory, e.g. Local Medical Committees, is also potentially difficult. Some chairmen have reported that being a member of both actually helps to defuse this potential for conflict between the demands of professional representation and views of needs versus that of spokesman for the local population. At this early stage this may be so; however, as decisions about development monies allocation begin to bite, the situation may change. There is a further tension inherent in the structure: the predominance of one professional group may make it very difficult for differing perceptions of the local population's needs to emerge or be heard (Harrison et al., 1992).

Setting Priorities

Another chairman spoke of this tension: 'I see my role as building up the Board, facilitating contributions, and focusing on the OD aspects, by keeping the wider agenda – inequalities and social exclusion, at the forefront.' This chairman was an exception to the prevailing view that as GPs, their own views of local needs were likely to be pretty accurate. As one commented:

> we've decided to look at things in terms of what are the real concrete problems that we've got and the real problems we've got are prescribing, costs and the ... policy issues. The other big one is bed blocking ...

This pragmatic approach conflicts with the longer term needs assessment and priority-setting processes which are more favoured by the centre.

Although each LHG has developed a performance agreement with its local HA spanning the next three years, specific priorities for the LHG itself have been harder to capture. The extent to which the priorities expressed are those of the chairman or are the result of work carried out by the Board – or indeed the result of examination of local needs – varied across all 22 LHGs. So, differing perceptions about both the role of LHGs and the appropriate process to identify needs, as well as what constitutes needs, is proving problematic.

A further challenge to effective local priority setting is the amount of work funnelling down from the centre to be dealt with at LHG level. As one chairman, commenting on his first six months in post, put it:

> I think we've had a reasonable time bedding in ... [but] we need to try to reduce
> the amount of paperwork we do for the Centre to meet Welsh Office guidelines
> and actually get down to business.

Clearly, Health Improvement Plans are the intended mechanism for identifying
and prioritising local needs, but the extent to which they have been a vehicle
for change in the first year was limited by the tight time-scale in which they
had to be produced, as well as by a perceived lack of LHG involvement in a
Health Authority-led process. These two factors have contributed to a feeling
among many that the whole exercise has been a paper-chase:

> I think Health Improvement Plans are basically things designed by public health
> physicians and bureaucrats and I mean yes it sounds very good and its all very
> important but in the real world it isn't something that's pre-eminent in your
> head ...

The widely held perception that LHGs need to be seen to be making a difference
on their patches, and doing so quickly, also militates against a longer range
strategic planning approach.

Creating Relationships with Stakeholder Agencies

New organisations need to be able to define their unique contribution to the
goals and aspirations of potential collaborators and customers if they are to
be able to persuade them of their added value. This might be through some
format for introducing themselves to their constituents. The first survey
revealed that few respondents had any concrete information about their LHG:
most could name neither the chairman or any GP members. Some LHGs (fewer
than half) have sent out an introductory newsletter/flyer to local practices.
Others opted for a personal approach and had instigated a series of visits,
either themselves or via their Clinical Governance lead, to introduce themselves
to local practices. Again this approach could be viewed as re-enforcing the
perception that LHGs are about GPs, or at best GP practices.

As for public involvement, the majority of LHG chairmen, though mindful
of the enormity of the task, left this to their lay representative to take forward.
There were three exceptions to this however, each of whom exercised a
community development approach. One used the opportunity of a local acute
services review to build a very effective alliance with the local population
which left the local politicians scrambling to jump on the LHG bandwagon.

Most, however, have done very little in this area; nor can the issue be said to have been particularly high on many chairmen's agendas at this stage.

A further challenge for these new organisations has been to create relationships with those who already occupy the territory. When this requires crossing long-standing community boundaries as well as professional ones, it is a challenging task. Creating LHGs coterminous with local authority boundaries may well help here. But where local authority boundaries contain significantly disparate socioeconomic groups, then creating agreement among local groups of GPs as to priorities in health needs may be difficult. Table 2.1 indicates the opportunities and challenges inherent in the new structures.

Secondary Sector

Trusts illustrate a complex set of relationships to be managed. Trusts have well established communication links with Health Authorities. As one Chairman put it: 'There is a six lane motorway running between the HA and the Trust. The little LHG mini-van can hardly get on the road ....' Trusts potentially share the same quality agenda as the LHG but the possibility exists to subvert that agenda for the Trust's own ends, and to play the LHGs and HAs off against each other. Examples of LHGs and Trusts working together do exist but they are in the minority. In one area, however, the hostilities were so hamstringing the LHG that the Chairman was thoroughly dispirited and contemplating resigning. More commonly, the Trusts are simply ignoring LHGs:

> ... they have their own agenda ... We haven't seen any sign that they are not developing along the lines that we have previously asked them not to, ... other priorities in cardiovascular or cancer services will be sidelined ....

It is probably fair to say that this potential conflagration has yet to be fanned. In these early days, before concrete disinvestment decisions are being contemplated, there is little to create disharmony – or harmony. Yet a real opportunity exists within national service frameworks and clinical pathways initiatives to create new and more appropriate service configurations. The incentives currently in the system to foster this may, however, be a bit subtle.

Health Authorities

Health Authority relationships with LHGs are particularly complex, containing a number of potentially conflicting levers as Table 2.1 shows. The cultural

Table 2.1 Relationships with key stakeholders: structural opportunities and challenges

Agency	Opportunities	Constraining factors
Health Authority	1 Access to resources: money and expertise 2 GM as HA appointee 3 Regular access to CEO and Executive Directors	1 Changing CEO postholders 2 Divided loyalties 3 Budgets retained at HA
Trusts	Shared agenda of local quality	Potential threat of disinvestment secondary to primary care
Local practices	1 Development funding agreed locally to meet local needs 2 Availability of local incentives 3 Potential conflict between development and monitoring functions	1 Proportion of GPFH on patch 2 Time and financial costs of involvement 3 Fear of loss of autonomy
Public/voluntary organisations	1 Potential resource in identification of local needs 2 Potential allies in creating shared public/professional agenda	1 Non-representativeness 2 Vocal minority of self interest
Local politicians	Potential allies in creating shared understanding of needs and availability of services	Potential threat of focusing on individual wants cf. population needs
National Assembly	1 Direct channel for communication of local needs 2 Referee cf. other local vested interests	1 Organisational capacity 2 Authority constrained by national UK agenda
Local professional representatives groups	Support profession's view of local needs and appropriate service responses	Desire to retain control over profession's 'voice' locally
Local Authorities	1 Coterminosity, so closer working relationships 2 Two LA representatives on LHG Board	Rivalry over who 'owns' the public health agenda
Local press/ media	Potential tool for re-educating public about local services and needs	Potential to twist agenda to emotive aspects cf. local wants

clash between GP chairmen hoping to make a difference, and to be seen to be doing so quickly, conflicts with the Health Authorities' slower approach to decision-making. Many chairmen voiced disappointment at the way issues, seemingly resolved at one HA Board meeting, would resurface for fresh debate several months later. Many chairmen also perceive a lack of direction. Some thrive in this ambiguity, but others find it less easy to work with, and feel hampered by an inability to make concrete progress. The main lever which might unlock this – budget control – has been the source of most frustration among chairmen across Wales.

As their first birthday approached, LHG chairmen in all but one Health Authority were complaining about the limitations lack of budget control has put on their organisations' ability to perform their roles. This is particularly acutely felt by ex-fundholder chairmen who are shocked by the strings attached to their notional budgets:

> [we need to] get a budget we can manipulate – no point in giving me a budget which is all tied up and gone, which is effectively what's happened this year … which, when you bear in mind all the money we had with all its flaws in fund-holding, is actually a retrograde step.

This plea was echoed at the most recent all-Wales Training session for LHG chairs in February and presented to Jane Hutt, Assembly Health Secretary. The alacrity with which Ms Hutt responded positively to the Chairmen's Group's request, in July, to meet quarterly was a real boost to morale. But Local Health Group chairmen will need to create effective communication channels with the Assembly if they are to succeed in getting their needs on the agenda, in the face of HA deficits and the national emphasis on waiting list initiatives. Here again, however, there may be questions as to Assembly members' collective understanding of the complex issues involved in the health arena (Williams, 1999).

Reimbursement for the role of chairman, compared to the time needed to do the job, is another source of real frustration and concern. The majority of chairmen reported giving more time to the role than reimbursement recognised. This imbalance was seen as creating palpable resentment within chairmen's own practices, and was a perceived problem by some retired chairmen, as well as those trying to fulfil their obligations to patients and partners. Many reported giving up their personal time in order to try to balance these conflicting demands. The guidance stated that chairmen should, preferably, be GPs (NHS Wales, 1998) but the reality is, that when push comes to shove, obligations to partners may carry the greatest priority. This prior loyalty may also be problematic in another respect: the GP chairmen can always pick up their bats and go home if and when the going gets tough. This security gives them an independence of outlook, which may clash with that of salaried public employees, leaving the latter stranded to pick up any pieces. At the same time, however, it may be that this very time pressure acts as a lever to push chairmen out of operational mode and into a more strategic one.

Conclusion: What Next?

This review of the first nine months of LHG activity as perceived by their chairmen has highlighted a number of potential problems inherent in the structuring of the new organisations. What support will the LHGs and the chairmen need to overcome these potential hurdles? There are a number of activities which could help LHGs to work more effectively.

Clinical governance: strengthening the extent to which clinical governance leads and chairmen work together could be a useful means of linking development to capacity and needs. Several chairmen noted that they left the CG Lead to work independently so as not to 'tread on his toes', but this reticence may make it harder to coordinate activity effectively.

Leadership: the chairmen may need external help to strengthen their own leadership capacity and strategic orientation. Specific issues about the development of a common vision, and facilitating the board's ability to work at policy not operational level may also benefit from external support.

Public involvement: strengthening the capacity for involving the public effectively is a need not currently being addressed. There is scope for effective involvement – and, indeed, potentially useful alliances to be made, in terms of needs assessment, priority setting and reconfiguration of services. There is a need for more identification and sharing of good practice across the service. It may be that a whole systems approach (Berwick, 1996), perhaps using clinical pathways, could help here.

Incentives: the incentives currently available are perceived as weak, yet scope for local initiatives in this arena certainly exists. Such incentives suitably applied could make a great deal of difference in the exercise of a developmental role and thereby help to foster the commitment of local GPs.

Budgets: first and foremost, clarity about budgets needs to be established between HAs and their LHGs. The perhaps unrealistic but nonetheless real expectations LHG chairmen have had over their ability to commit resources has been a source of continuous frustration leading to demoralisation in some cases.

Development criteria: clear criteria to enable LHGs to develop, measure and monitor their own organisational capacity and readiness to progress to subsequent levels need to be established as soon as possible. Without this, they are inevitably going to founder.

Acknowledgements

Grateful thanks are due to the 22 LHG chairmen who so generously gave their time to be interviewed, and to the 80 GPs who responded to the first survey.

References

Berwick, D. (1996), 'A Primer on Leading the Improvement of Systems', *British Medical Journal*, 312, pp. 619–22.

Department of Health (1989), *Working for Patients*, HMSO, London.

Department of Health: NHS Wales (1998), *Putting Patients First*, HMSO: London.

Harrison, S., Hunter, D.J., Marnoch, G. and Pollitt, C. (1992), *Just Managing: Power and culture in the National Health Service*, Macmillan Press Ltd, Basingstoke.

Henry, S. (1999), 'Under the Volcano', *Health Management*, 3 (2), pp. 16–17.

NHS Wales (1998), *Establishing Local Health Groups*, Welsh Office, Cardiff.

NHS Wales (1999), 'The Health Responsibilities of the National Assembly for Wales: Organisational preparations', WHC (99) 73, April.

Williams, K. (1999), presentation to MSc in Health Service Management students, UWCM, 12 November.

Chapter Three

Developing an Organisation Made up of People who Thrive on Change

Sue Phillips, Oliver Nyumbu and Brian Toner

Introduction

The central concern of this chapter is to explore the challenge of designing, implementing and reviewing a management development programme to enhance leadership capacity. The ultimate goal is to ensure organisational effectiveness within a rapidly changing external environment. To that end the programme aims to enhance the innovation capacity and the adaptive capability of managers.

As it is used here, innovation can be defined as 'an idea, practice, or object that is perceived as new by an individual or another unit of adoption' (Rogers, 1995, p. xviii). As such, innovation can be a result of or a trigger for change. A key notion in Roger's definition is the word '*new*'. We shall return to this idea later in the chapter.

Just as important as the idea of innovation capacity, is that of adaptive capability by which, if we were successful in developing this capability in our managers, would mean that they:

> adapt more successfully to their environments, given their purposes and values, by facing painful circumstances and developing new attitudes and behaviours. They learn to distinguish reality from fantasy, resolve internal conflicts, and put harsh events into perspective. They learn to live with things that cannot be changed and take responsibility for those that can (Heifetz, 1995, p. 5).

This idea of adaptive capability is important for several reasons. First, as much as suffering the effects of current changes, managers can face difficulties because of having procrastinated on responses to other changes in the recent past. This could be a function of inappropriate contentment or denial. Second,

Organisation Development in Health Care: Strategic Issues in Health Care Management, R.K. Rushmer, H.T.O. Davies, M. Tavakoli and M. Malek (eds), Ashgate Publishing Ltd, 2002.

managers could out of confusion (too many questions or options) attempt too much. Much like the grief curve, Janssen (in Weisbord, 1987), a social psychologist, conceptualises this problem as a four-room apartment whose rooms we visit or occupy in times of change (see Figure 3.1). We have modified Janssen's model to include trap doors and a work room/construction site.

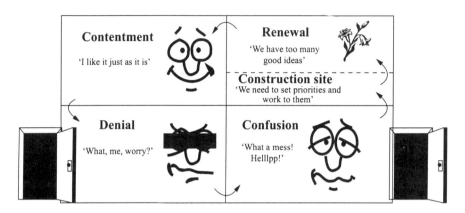

Source: Nyumbu, 1999, based on Claes Janssen in Weisbord, 1987.

Figure 3.1   The extended four-room apartment

It was one of our working hypotheses that before, during and after a management development programme, managers would inevitably experience a roller coaster, which would take them through the rooms of Janssen's model. It followed therefore that they needed both adaptive strategies, to cope with current reality and emergent situations, and innovation skills and strategies with which to make the most of change.

The development of innovation capacity and adaptive capability had, in our view, two important implications: effective management of change and effective transfers of training so it would translate into workplace behaviours. Neither change management nor transfer of training have a good track record. Many major change programmes, over 75 per cent according to Boydell and Leary (1996) and other researchers, fail. The reason for this, Boydell and Leary argue, is that on the whole, these programmes fail to take a holistic view of all the systems (technical, human, financial, etc.) and fail to encompass a broad enough range of stakeholders.

This last point echoes what Weisbord (1987) calls the 'learning curve', by which he contends that in the 1900s 'experts' solved problems, while in the 1950s 'everybody', in organisations, solved problems. From about 1965, he argues, 'experts' improved whole systems, while the 2000s will witness 'everybody' improving whole systems. Consistent with this view, Weisbord offers four practical guidelines for effecting change through helping people learn:

- assess the potential for action;
- get the whole system in the room;
- focus on the future;
- structure tasks people can do for themselves.

The problem of effective transfer of learning to the workplace is well established (Robinson and Robinson, 1995; Baldwin and Ford, 1988). Indeed, Baldwin and Ford conclude that on average only 10 to 20 per cent of training transfers to the job so as to change performance and that not more than 10 per cent of expenditure on training and development, up to $100 bn in America for example, actually results in transfer to the job. This and other research seems to confirm the assertion of earlier work (Mosel, 1957, pp. 56–64), which pointed to 'mounting evidence that showed that very often the training makes little or no difference in job behaviour'.

Implementation

The overall aim of the management development programme, in addition to developing adaptive capacity, was to provide everyone who has managerial responsibility in our organisation with a common language to describe key organisational features and a common understanding of the organisation in which we work. Mental Health Services for Older Adults (MHSOA) is one of three Directorates in a Mental Health Trust serving half the population of Birmingham, the second largest city in the UK. Our clients are primarily people over the age of 65 who have developed mental health needs requiring support from secondary care services.

We form a small part of a larger NHS Trust and are constantly fighting to draw attention to the needs of a neglected client group (Audit Commission, 2000). We hold awards for excellence and amongst agencies dealing with older people in the city are held in relatively high regard. As part of the NHS we must work to guidelines, policies and initiatives imposed on us by the Department of Health (DoH). Department of Health imperatives are non-negotiable and we have only a small voice in shaping them. One effect of this organisational environment is that MHSOA staff feel that they are under constant pressure to change, and that much of this change is driven by financial demands.

It is against this backdrop that the development programme was designed, a key objective being to develop a capacity to handle change in such a way that the Directorate would be able to seize those opportunities that allow us to determine our own future within the constraints of NHS funding and DoH directives. We recognised at the outset that our long-term future depends on our ability to pursue change strategically and productively. Being aware of the limitations of standard development programmes as described above (Broad and Newstrom, 1992: Robinson and Robinson, 1995; Baldwin and Ford, 1988; Mosel, 1957), we chose to devise a model that would both promote change as a positive process and develop the expectation in our staff that they should play a part in determining our service's future.

We identified 50 key players from our staff of around 300 and targeted them for involvement in a programme of development that would take place over the course of a year. We wanted to assure maximum engagement of these managers in the learning process. To do this we decided the content of the programme should be delivered entirely by our own staff. The process would be supported by a facilitator brought in from outside our organisation. The role of the facilitator was to inform us of developments external to our own service and sector, and to act as an enabler during the training sessions.

Four themes were chosen as generic conceptual handles for working with change. The themes are: organisations; change; teams, and developing people. The broad outline for each topic area was designed by the service director and quality manager, both of whom were relatively new to MHSOA but each of whom brought considerable training experience to the organisation. From the outset we agreed that participation in the programme should be an enjoyable experience for everyone. The structure provided three distinct learning opportunities; the preparation period, the two-day residential course, and a follow up programme. During the first year the follow up programme would have two formal components: a cascade process and review workshops.

The idea for the programme was introduced to the target audience by letter, though the proposal had already been submitted to the Directorate Board and its goals, purpose and format included in the minutes. The first course would be a pilot. The most senior person from each area of the service would be included as a participant, and would play a part in determining its future, evaluating the content, method and structure. This gave us a group of 15 people which included the 'core management team', clinical director, service director, clinical services manager, support services manager and quality manager, senior nurses from inpatient and community services, head of professions allied to medicine (PAMs), head of psychology and pharmacy and a lead Consultant Psychiatrist. The Trust personnel manager was also invited as a full participant. In the event medical representation was limited to evening participation by the clinical director, but all the other managers were fully involved in the process.

Involvement of the first 15 managers began with a briefing about the four themes, and an invitation for each participant to select one of the themes to research. The programme was to take place over two days at a venue removed from the normal working environment but not far from base, or from home. Everyone was expected to stay overnight and involvement in some evening activities was mandatory. But engagement did not start or end here. Prior to the residential component each person prepared a contribution to the content within his or her selected theme. The service director and the quality manager each supervised (we adopted the term 'champion' for this role) two themes and gave support to participants in their planning and preparation. Support took the form of advice on sources of information and coordination of content and method of learning. Sound theory, variety of presentation and fun were all criteria used by the two champions.

The first programme was a resounding success. Though anxiety had been running high throughout because of the pressure to perform in front of peers, the blend of theory, reflection and challenge left everyone feeling extremely positive about the experience. The discovery of hidden talents amongst their peers aided by the mixture of teaching methods left everyone feeling invigorated by the experience. The facilitator, who as an outside agent had been viewed by some as a threat, proved his worth by providing the missing links when the content showed signs of being disconnected. The insights he was able to provide from his extensive experience in both public and private sector bodies helped to contextualise our homespun material in a very powerful way.

The final session on Day 2 was a discussion that was decisive in establishing the roll out of the programme. The group unanimously recommended that:

- the programme should be rolled out to include all 50 managers, plus consultants;
- each programme should be multidisciplinary;
- each programme should be residential;
- each programme should involve all participants in delivering part of the content;

- a champion for each topic area should be appointed from among participants at the previous course;
- each programme should be facilitated by an external facilitator.

Evaluation sheets were distributed, and people were asked to return them after a period of reflection. Some were never returned, and we learned from this that if feedback was to be anonymous we should give out the sheets at the start of the course and collect them in at the end.

Details of the programme are shown in Figure 3.2. Handouts were produced from the materials used, including descriptions of the exercises as well as the theoretical content. These became a resource for the four champions who undertook to take the lead for the second programme.

The second course took place three months later and everything seemed set to ensure a near perfect roll out. Until the third programme, which was when we began to experience the undesirable outcomes of the cascade process. Feedback from participants via the evaluation sheets gave one indication.

Mean scores on both enjoyment and relevance were marginally lower, as shown in Table 3.1.

Table 3.1   Mean scores on enjoyment and relevance taken from end of course evaluation sheets

	Interest mean score	Interest standard deviation	Relevance mean score	Relevance standard deviation
Course 1	8.3	0.448	7.6	0.535
Course 2	7.9	0.994	7.6	1.174
Course 3	7.5	0.905	7.25	0.965
Total	7.8	0.889	7.5	0.948

However, the more compelling criticisms came from the programme manager (quality manager) and the facilitator who were able to compare all three courses, and could be detected in the responses made by participants to the question on the evaluation sheet that asked about the organisation of the event.

Three examples from each of the courses showing a gradual shift towards loss of focus are given in Table 3.2.

Learning from our Mistakes

A number of observations contributed to our learning and have been embedded

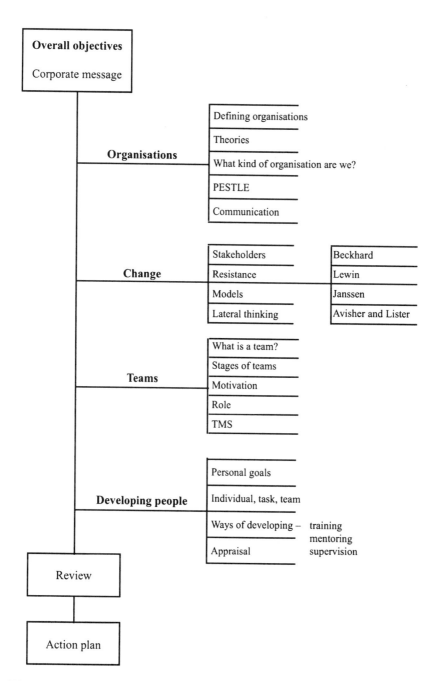

Figure 3.2   Programme framework

Table 3.2   Sample answers to the question what did you think of the organisation of the event?

Course 1	Course 2	Course 3
Sessions were well planned and covered relevant subjects, timing was well planned. I was very impressed with the input and participation	Excellent. Congratulations to whoever thought this method up; having everyone contribute enriched the whole process	I felt the individual/group presentations contained too many similar exercises, and these would benefit from more variation
Well organised, well planned and people knew what was expected of them	Thoroughly enjoyable and informative both in terms of course content and networking. Novel way of involving course members in presenting a course mentored by champions	Perhaps a little more groundwork prior to attending would help teams work cooperatively
Exceptional!	It was good but there was some repetition, which may not have been a problem. Perhaps some coordination between the different groups might have been beneficial	Would have preferred more information distributed sooner

in the planning for the fourth course. Criticisms levelled against cascade methods of training generally include the fact that the method fails to deliver continuity of learning. It is our observation that the programme requires more in the way of supportive infrastructure than we first envisaged. At the outset we had resisted stifling creativity by imposing too much control over the detail and delivery of the programme content. However at this point we were forced to review our stance. A balance needed to be maintained between being totally prescriptive on the one hand and facilitating a pooling of ignorance on the other. A number of steps have been taken in preparation for the fourth programme:

- the course framework (as per Figure 3.2) has been made explicit to champions and participants at the preparation stage, as opposed to being emergent within the review;
- learning packs including suggested exercises have been provided to the next set of champions for distribution to participants;
- a schedule for meetings between champions has been circulated as part of the advance information.

Although we are confident that we will see benefits resulting from these three steps, our realism tells us that even this will not produce a foolproof solution to the problem of coordination. As providers of an inpatient and community mental health service we experience the knock on effects of staff sickness on inpatient units for example, on all planned meetings. So the schedule is supplemented by roving support from the Programme Manager (quality manager) and loads of patient telephoning and e-mailing by the Training Coordinator.

Successes to Report

The difficulty of setting aside time for nonoperational activities in a busy and stretched service has had an impact on our planned series of 'refresher' sessions. To date we have held only one. It was originally envisaged that we would hold quarterly events focusing on current issues for people who already had developed a shared vocabulary in the form of the models we had included in each programme. The one event held to date provided reinforcement on the value of the models of change that had been included within the programme. There was good evidence of the transfer from theory to practice in the context of a particularly demanding series of changes connected with restructuring parts of the service.

Future events are planned but with a greater degree of realism taking into consideration the competing demands on people's time. Despite this modification to our plans, a survey of all participants of the programme undertaken between three and nine months after people had participated in the programme has shown a high level of enthusiasm for the programme. All participants were invited to describe a maximum of three benefits they had experienced personally; three benefits experienced by their staff; three reservations or criticism they held personally; and three reservations or criticism held by their staff. Over 80 per cent of participants who were still employed in the service responded. Some respondents listed only positive comments, and some did not feel able to respond from the perspective of their staff. However, over 140 independent comments were made to the four questions. Construct analysis enabled us to cluster these comments into 21 subgroups. A description of the constructs and the percentage of responses within each of the four categories is shown in Table 3.3.

This second level evaluation is considered by many (e.g. Hamblin, 1971) as more valuable than immediate feedback. In practical terms the negative

Table 3.3   Responses to a post-course questionnaire asking four open-ended questions

List the top three	Constructs described	% responses
Benefits I have experienced personally	Opportunity for reflection/learning	45%
	Building and developing relationships	39%
	Being valued has had impact on my performance	8%
Total responses = 66	New insights into colleagues and self	5%
	Organisational gains	3%
	Improved relationships	25%
Benefits experience by my staff	Wider perspective on our organisation	21%
	Team goals	18%
	Increased confidence in me as a manager	14%
Total responses = 28	Being valued by the organisation	14%
	Learning on specific topics	7%
Reservations/criticisms held personally	Inadequate/incomplete follow up	41%
	Lack of clarity/direction during course	31%
	Difficult feelings generated	17%
Total responses = 28	Inadequate preparation before course	10%
	Waste of resources	21%
Reservations/criticisms held by my staff	General negative comments	21%
	They'd like the opportunity to go too	16%
	Anxiety about making presentations	16%
Total responses = 19	Practical problems	16%
	Lack of clarity over next steps	10%

feedback has strengthened our determination to exercise more control over the cascade process for the fourth course, whilst the positive comments map onto our original goals of giving us:

• a common language to describe key organisational features;
• a common understanding of the organisation in which we work;
• improved adaptive capacity, especially in terms of the way people understand and manage change.

An additional gain that was articulated by over two-thirds of respondents is the way involvement in the programme enabled them to build and develop relationships with a wider group of people. This was expressed by one core team member as, 'Having opportunity to work alongside staff whom I would not normally have that sort of contact, often grass roots staff see you as a name on a page.'

Discussion

As outlined above, the programme can be considered a success, in terms of innovation capacity, adaptive capability and transfer of learning, as judged by participants and observed by the programme manager. This is partly explained by the facilitation of what Caine and Caine (1997) call dynamical knowledge, which contrasts with technical knowledge. Most significantly, dynamical knowledge connects to the real knowledge of the learner as one senior manager reported, 'I championed the topic teamworking. The preparation and research for the subject increased my knowledge base. This in turn has assisted me greatly in my day to day work.' The structure itself offered a model dynamically applied by at least one participant who described one of the benefits experienced by her staff thus: ' I applied the "champion" approach to work related topics.'

This evidence for dynamical knowledge was, we believe, achieved through the combination of direction and self-direction. The direction was provided by the course designers through areas of course content, duration and timing of the course. The course objectives were also predetermined but the course manager and facilitator invited the participants to negotiate on this as well. Brookfield (1996, p. 216) observes that 'there can be no other alternative to this process of negotiation, change and alteration' if learning is to occur.

This negotiation was not easy but important if the course was to help participants develop their capabilities for change and adaptive capability. The difficulty lay, in part, in the need to promise value for money at the start of the course while seeking to avoid or minimise the danger that 'the predetermined objectives approach represents an implicit alignment by educators with systems of control and authority in society' (Brookfield, 1996, p. 215; see also Jones, 1982; Robinson and Taylor, 1983). We did not want to merely deliver information and ask the participants to memorise facts and techniques.

This approach tested our own adaptive capability as we observed a gradual loss of focus between course one and three (see Table 3.2 above). In part this is because knowledge is socially constructed and as the adult learners, the participants, learned together before, during, and after the two-day residential course, much unplanned and incidental learning took place. Evidently, it is not possible for course managers or facilitators to anticipate or predetermine all the learning before it occurs (Apps, 1981). Thus it became clear to us that on its own, technical knowledge (and rigidly predetermined learning objectives) would be insufficient for our situation:

It [technical or scholastic knowledge] is extremely important, irrespective of whether it is acquired in school or elsewhere; but it is limited because technical or scholastic knowledge, by itself, excludes what Gardner calls 'generative' or 'deep' or 'genuine' understanding. That is, scholastic knowledge lacks a quality that makes it available for solving problems or for dealing with complex situations (Caine and Caine, 1997, p. 31).

It was, in part, a pursuit of the balance between technical knowledge and dynamical knowledge that contributed to the success of the course.

A second possible explanation for the success of the course is to do with the non-negotiable requirement that every participant would work with at least two others and a champion to prepare and present on one of the four areas of study. This meant that participants were not coming as either passive receptacles of knowledge or only to participate through asking one or two questions. Therefore even before the course they were addressing themselves to the structure of the knowledge on their chosen topic and to what and where were the key works and theorists. In this way their practice challenged theory while theory informed practice. By their own admission, this meant that the participants had an energising sense of responsibility for the course and its success. They for instance felt it important to support and critique colleagues so they could themselves receive similar help when it was their turn.

Key adult learning methods such as use of discussion, lectures from colleagues, demonstrations and independent study have turned out to be our third critical component. The discussion experienced in the course can be defined as 'directed conversation on a topic of mutual interest' (Brunner et al., 1959, in Brookfield, 1996, p. 38) and 'a conversation with a purpose' (Brown, 1975, in Brookfield, 1996, p. 138). It was important that participants were able to talk freely (Legge, 1971). This last requirement of discussion was especially challenging to the facilitators. Were they to act merely as process managers? Indeed this did from time to time cause confusion for some participants. How were the facilitators to enable participants to undertake the typically threatening re-evaluation of their own values and behaviours while avoiding the kind of paralysing block often associated with this aspect of adult learning? This challenge demonstrated the value of shared facilitation; the facilitators could 'compare notes' and ensure course correction if necessary. This balance between the group's needs for effective discussion on the one hand and effective facilitation on the other played a critical role in keeping the course effective.

Acknowledgements

Our thanks to all MHSOA participating staff whose willingness to take risks enabled us to test out our hypotheses.

References

Apps, J.W. (1981), *The Adult Learner on Campus: A Guide for Instructors and Administrators*, Cambridge Books, New York.

Audit Commission (2000), *Forget me not – Mental Health Services for Older People*, Audit Commission for Local Authorities and the National Health Service in England and Wales, London.

Baldwin, T.T. and Ford, K.K. (1988), 'Transfer of Training: A Review and Directions for future Research', *Personnel Psychology*, 41, pp. 63–105.

Borrill, C. and Haynes, C. (2000), 'Stress to Kill', *Health Service Journal*, 10 (2), pp. 24–5.

Boydell, T. and Leary, M. (1996), *Identifying Training Needs*, Institute of Personnel and Development, London.

Broad, M.L. and Newstrom, J.W. (1992), *Transfer of Training*, Addison-Wesley, Massachusetts.

Brookfield, S.D. (1996), *Understanding and Facilitating Adult Learning*, Open University Press, Milton Keynes, England.

Brown, G. (1975), *Microteaching: A Programme of Teaching Skills*, London, Methuen.

Brunner, E. de S. et al. (1959), *An Overview of Adult Education Research*, Adult Education Association of the USA, Chicago.

Caine, R.N. and Caine, G. (1997), *Unleashing the Power of Perceptual Change*, ASCD, Virginia.

Hamblin, A.C. (1971), *Evaluation and Control of Training*, McGraw-Hill, London.

Heifetz, R.A. (1995), *Leadership Without Easy Answers*, Harvard University Press, Boston, Mass.

Jones, R.K. (1982), 'The Dilemma of Educational Objectives in Higher and Adult Education: Do We Need Them?', *Adult Education* (USA), 32 (3), pp. 165–9.

Legge, D. (1971), *Relationships within Adult Classes*, in M.D. Stephens and G.W. Roderick (eds), Teaching Techniques in Adult Education, David and Charles, Newton Abbot.

Mosel, J.N. (1957), 'Why Training Programmes Fail to Carry Over', *Personnel*, 34, pp. 56–64.

Robinson, D.G. and Robinson, J.C. (1995), *Performance Consulting: Moving Beyond Training*, Berrett-Koehler, San Francisco.

Robinson, J.J. and Taylor, D. (1983), 'Behavioural Objectives in Training for Adult Education', *International Journal of Lifelong Education*, 2 (4), pp. 355–69.

Rogers, E.M. (1995), *Diffusion of Innovations*, The Free Press, New York.

Weisbord, M.R. (1987), *Productive Workplaces: Organizing and Managing for Dignity, Meaning and Community*, Jossey-Bass, San Francisco.

SECTION TWO
TEAMS AND
INTERDISCIPLINARY
WORKING

Chapter Four

Introducing Self-Directed Primary Care Teams in the NHS: An Overview of Initial Strategic Issues

Rosemary K. Rushmer, Julia Parker and Sheila Phillips

Overview of the Project

What follows are details of a project designed to produce empowerment amongst staff working within Primary Care in the National Health Service (NHS) in the UK. The chapter gives an overview of the project, its goals, issues raised in the planning process and details the evaluation study that will track its progress.

Background

The UK Government White Papers 'Designed to Care' and (in Scotland) 'Towards a New Way of Working' (Scottish Office Department of Health, 1998a, 1998b), identify empowerment, participation and flatter team-based structures as the way forward for the NHS in its fiftieth year and beyond. From the newly devolved government in Scotland, the Executive Planning and Priorities Guidance committee for the NHS states that, within primary care, the development of SDTs is to be a national objective. In response to this, Dundee Local Health Care Cooperative (LHCC), as part of Tayside Primary Care Trust, is seeking to establish self-directed primary care (SDPC) teams. Unique in the UK, the project seeks to establish a SDPC team across disciplines: GPs, practice nurses, community nurses, PAMs, administrative staff and with the future inclusion of social workers across employers and agencies.

Organisation Development in Health Care: Strategic Issues in Health Care Management, R.K. Rushmer, H.T.O. Davies, M. Tavakoli and M. Malek (eds), Ashgate Publishing Ltd, 2002.

Literature

Research into the desirability and efficacy of self-directed teams is mixed and has typically concentrated on teamworking under one employer. In the private sector, teams are claimed to enhance integration, cooperation, job satisfaction and productivity (Teresko, 1996; Buchanan, 1994). However, contrary claims identify work intensification and increasing management control (Parker and Slaughter, 1988; Procter and Mueller, 2000). There is generally a lack of rigorous team research in the NHS (exceptions are West, 1995; West and Slater, 1995). What data does exist is similarly split between positive and negative messages; however, evidence in favour of teams is often anecdotal and rarely independent. Jones Elwyn et al. (1998) claim that primary care teams in the NHS are undesirable and unnecessary, they offer time limited project teams as an alternative. Others argue that the introduction of teams is unwelcome by NHS employees because for some it may threaten the 'privileged' status that the present order affords them (Bartkus, 1997). McHugh (1995) argues that while teamworking is highly desirable in theory, it is extremely difficult to effect in practice because of the joint constraints of time and working practices making meetings difficult. A similar theme is pursued by Hunter (1996), who claims that 'tribal' barriers between different health professionals will prove difficult to overcome in practice and thus will prove a persistent barrier to effective teamworking in the NHS.

The Project

Agencies Involved

This project is being undertaken by Dundee LHCC as part of Tayside Primary Care Trust and fully supported by Tayside Social Work Department.

Project Mission

To provide leadership and support to enable primary care teams to improve their performance through effective teamwork, personal development of members and empowerment through the context of self-direction.

Project Goals

1   To create an effective development and empowerment process for the use of participating primary care teams.
2   To enable Dundee primary care teams to improve their performance in key areas including patient care, efficiency, employee skills and employee satisfaction through the utilisation of the process in partnership with other local service personnel and other agencies.
3   To ensure the project is aligned with the HIP (health improvement plan) and TIP (Tayside implementation plan) process.
4   To engage all primary care teams in the project by the year 2005.

Self-Directed Team Definition

The following definition provided guidance in the planning of the project:

> A group of employees who are responsible for delivering a whole service or process. The team plans the work, perform it, managing many of the things supervision or management used to do. The team meets regularly to identify, analyse, and solve problems. They may set schedules, goals, give performance feedback, recruitment, and dismissal etc. The team's duties grow with their skills. Different teams take in different ranges of responsibilities and normally on an incremental basis.

The Team and its Tasks

After planning and consultation an important alteration was made to the above definition. It was decided, for the sake of fostering cooperative relationships, discipline would not be handled with the teams. The performance management tasks that were to be made available to the team were as follows:

- recruitment and selection;
- prioritisation of work and goal setting;
- managing absence;
- appraisal;
- training budgets;
- staffing budgets;
- consumables budgets.

The above tasks will only be devolved at a pace that is decided by the team. Training and consultation with the central support structures of the Trust is an integral part of the process.

Within the remit of this project, the team itself decides the exact membership of the new self-directed team. To date teams are selecting all members of the practice that are involved in service provision (which includes service delivery and service organisation). This makes the initial composition of the team range across health professions including GP's, all nurses, PAMs (professions allied to medicine e.g. physiotherapy, dietetics, occupational therapy, chiropody etc.) and administrative staff. Additionally, as well as being multidisciplinary, the team will cross employers and eventually, with the cooperation of social workers, it will bridge agencies involved in the provision of health and social welfare.

Participation and Involvement of Stakeholders in the Planning Stage

As an exercise in empowerment and democratisation in the NHS, the planning group was established in late 1998, to involve representatives from all major stakeholder groups (Dundee LHCC; Tayside Primary Care Trust; Tayside Social Work Department; nurse management; GPs; practice nurses; health visitors; district nurses; practice managers; PAMs representatives; community pharmacy; union representation). Because of the resource implications involved in successfully supporting the programme (training, locum cover, facilitation etc.) it was decided to phase the introduction of the project. At a public launch, all practices eligible for participation (more than 30 in all) were invited to attend and discuss the project. Following this, volunteer practices were sought to take part in Phase One of the introduction of the project. Five practices were selected from the volunteers. To date these practice are just beginning their 'teaming' training with off-site time-protected training events.

The Evaluation Study

This study will critically (and independently) track the form and process of the initiative during its first three years of implementation. Assessing the project's success in terms of evaluating the strategic and operational steps taken to achieve the project goals and to avoid the 'teamworking pitfalls' as identified by the literature.

Method

Different methods are being employed in order to identify present ways of working (both qualitative and quantitative) and examine resultant changes against them:

- interviews with key stakeholders;
- application of a behaviourally anchored rating scale (BARS) questionnaire on teamworking;
- identification of critical incidents which facilitate or hinder project progress;
- case study mapping the content and process of planning and implementation
- sociograms identifying changes in communication flow through the hierarchy;
- identification of blockages in order to streamline the process of care delivered to patients by the teams, i.e. simplifying the patients journey (service process re-engineering).

Results

The research is in its early stages and the data collection is ongoing. Further papers will report findings and address research implications.

Initial Issues Arising During Planning

A Team Across Employers

For some community staff, there was concern that this initiative simply marked a shift in who 'controlled' them. Some saw it as the beginning of a handover from a management system led by the Trust to one led by the GPs through the practice manager. However, the aim of the project is simply to create autonomy within the primary care team to allow practitioners to make decisions related to service provision for themselves as professions. Decision-making is to move to the team and not simply from the Trust hierarchy to the practice hierarchy. Fear versus trust are factors that will determine the pace and the distance that empowerment attempts will travel.

A second issue here is that within a team: if decision-making is to be embraced by all members; then all members have to feel free to express their opinions. With some members of staff (practice nurses and administrative staff) held within a 'line' relationship with other members of the team (practice manager and GPs), some felt it difficult to be open and honest in their opinions. Across employers and agencies, loyalties will be divided within the team, this may curtail free involvement by all team members.

A third issue here concerned the GPs as independent business people. With money invested in their staff, buildings and with the ultimate responsibility for health care provision resting with them, some felt that theirs should be the loudest voice.

A Team Across Agencies

Decisions about bridging agencies through teamworking was an issue that could not be approached by each team individually in an ad hoc way. Policy and protocol had to be formed at strategic level in order to form a working alliance between TCPT and Tayside Social Work Department. In this way some issues emerged, that it was not appropriate to empower the teams to perform. In these instances, it was much more efficient and effective to have a central body to act on behalf of the teams.

Coherence and Consistency of Service Provision

As its central tenet, the project has the desire to empower NHS staff, to take forward service provision and professional practice. Primary care teams need to be aware of the particular needs of the client group that their practice serves and make their service provision sensitive to it. Ironically, through empowerment, by allowing staff to take discretion over their own service delivery, the whole coherence and consistency of the NHS could be threatened. If each practice is allowed to go off and 'do its own thing' then the coherence of the area wide service provision runs the risk of fragmenting as service provision becomes dictated by postcode, or rather care is dictated by the particular practice to which one is signed up.

Integration of Service Provision

Another threat inherent in the change programme to the central NHS is the potential for the service to become disjointed and integration of service provision across geographical areas could be endangered. For example, one practice could respond to a vacancy in their staffing levels by altering the number of hours dedicated to a particular nursing discipline (and change the grade at which the new employee is to work). This may suit the team in question very well; however, this could run counter to the interests of a neighbouring practice, which needs shared cover. Integration and reciprocal cover arrangements could be compromised.

The Ripple Effect

The programme aims to alter the organisation and working of primary care teams. However, like dropping a stone into water, the effects spread. As the teams begin to have greater involvement in recruitment, appraisals and accessing and 'controlling' their budgets, so central departments will have to start working differently to facilitate this. The human resource department will have to learn to devolve its skills and expertise to facilitate the team's new work and the finance department will have to learn to let go of public money. Immediately this raises questions of public accountability and audit trails etc.

Conclusion: Limits to Empowerment?

Most of the above could be categorised under the broad heading of *limits to empowerment*. Against the basic vision of the programme, it became obvious that to preserve integration between the teams in the NHS and conserve coherence and consistency in service delivery, empowerment had its limits. For strategic coherence, *what* was identified as priorities had to be set centrally; *how* this was to achieved was to be left to the discretion of the teams. As well as the reasons above, the realisation grew that within primary care the 'team' is too small and isolated a unit within the organisation to direct policy for the whole of the NHS. Basically, each team was to be empowered to act on issues that affected their team, but where the issue was one that was held in common with other team(s) and across other NHS units, consultation rather than unilateral individual team action had to be the norm.

It was decided to let members of the self-directed teams form a 'forum' to discuss issues that affected them all in common and on which their vision and information was too narrow to take a decision alone. Strategic guidance and parameters to the empowerment process were provided with the health improvement plan (HIP) and the Tayside Implementation Plan (TIP) and each local practice development plan (PDP). Rather than the planned 'bottom-up' change programme that was envisioned, the project will follow a 'top-led, bottom-fed' approach.

The Contribution of the Study

In light of the initial issues arising (above), the focus of the study, its data collection and critical debate will be addressed to the following issues:

- identification of the issues involved in establishing successful multi-agency teams (individual, organisational and strategic);
- evaluation of the desirability, practicality and likely acceptance and adoption of the changes proposed;
- to locate what degree of autonomy can be permitted to these teams to innovate service delivery and be sensitive to local needs whilst maintaining consistency in service deliver across practices and coherency of the wider NHS (and social work) strategies in general (i.e. how self-directing and autonomous are the 'central NHS/social work' able to let these teams become);
- delineate the changes necessary in the central bureaucracy and management structures of the NHS (and social work) in order to allow for a degree of 'decentralisation' and autonomy to the teams;
- specify management controls that need to accompany decentralisation of 'care in the community' in order to preserve public accountability;
- to assess what impact these changes might have on future government policy on partnership, social inclusion, multi-agency working in the community and cost containment thereof.

References

Bartkus, B. (1997), 'Employee Ownership as a Catalyst of Organizational Change', *Journal of Organizational Change Management*, 10, 4, pp. 331–44.

Buchanan, D. (1994), 'Cellular Manufacturing and the Role of Teams', in J. Storey (ed.), *New Wave Manufacturing Strategies*, Paul Chapman, London, pp. 204–25.

Hunter, D.J. (1996), 'The Changing Roles of Health Personnel in Health and Health Care Management.', *Social Science and Medicine*, 43, pp. 799–808.

Jones Elwyn, G., Rapport, F. and Kinnersley, P. (1998), 'Primary Health Care Teams Re-Engineered', *Journal of Interprofessional Care*, 2, 12, pp. 189–98.

McHugh, M. (1995), 'Stress and Strategic Change', D. in Hussey (ed.), *Rethinking Strategic Management*, John Wiley and Sons, Chichester.

Parker, M. and Slaughter, J. (1988), *Choosing Sides: Unions and the Team Concept*, South End Press, Boston.

Procter, S. and Mueller, F. (2000), *Teamworking*, Management Work and Organisations series, Macmillan Business, Basingstoke.

Scottish Office Department of Health (1998a), *Designed to Care: Renewing the National Health Service in Scotland*, Cmd 3811, The Stationery Office, Edinburgh.

Scottish Office Department of Health (1998b), *Towards a New Way of Working – the Plan for Managing People in the NHS in Scotland*, April, The Stationery Office, Edinburgh.

Teresko, J. (1996), 'American Best Plants', *Industry Week*, 245, 19, p. 50.

West, M. (1995), *The Effectiveness of Teamworking in Primary Health Care. A Report to the Health Education Authority*, Sheffield, Institute of Work Psychology.

West, M. and Slater, J. (1995), 'Teamwork, Myths, Realities and Research', *The Occupational Psychologist*, 24, pp. 24–9.

Chapter Five

Interprofessional Education: One Aspect of Achieving Quality Health and Social Care

Anne Wyness, Brian O'Neill, Sharon McKinnon, Peter Granger, Irene Goldstone, Robert Martel, Andrew Chalmers and Paul Perchal

Introduction

Providing health care services today is a complex undertaking (Tresolini and the Pew-Fetzer Task Force on Advancing Psychosocial Health Education, 1994). Effective and efficient collaboration across professional boundaries is necessary to meet the needs of the diverse populations served by modern health care systems. To achieve such collaboration in practice, changes are needed in both the service delivery structure and the preparation of professionals (Brandon and Knapp, 1999). Due to demographic and social changes in the population, care providers must be sensitive and responsive to differences related not only to age and gender, but also to socioeconomic class, ethnicity, culture, language, religion and sexual orientation. Individuals are living longer and presenting multifaceted care needs. Furthermore, many health care recipients are better educated as consumers and expect to participate actively in health care decisions (Owen, 1998). Hence, practitioners need to be culturally competent, having an understanding of the meanings of health and health care for diverse groups (Green, 1999) as well as the patterns of disease and its treatment in various populations (Lavizzo-Mourey and MacKenzie, 1995). Certain illnesses, for example HIV, particularly impact marginalised populations in North America and Europe, and require the intervention of teams of professionals.

The provision of health care is also complex due to changes within the service delivery system itself. A philosophy of holistic care, an emphasis on outcome-based standards, and pressure to make efficient use of resources are

Organisation Development in Health Care: Strategic Issues in Health Care Management, R.K. Rushmer, H.T.O. Davies, M. Tavakoli and M. Malek (eds), Ashgate Publishing Ltd, 2002.

shaping the system (Almgren, 1998). Coordination and integration of services, often by means of managed care, are seen as ways of achieving these goals. In addition, as a result of the increased participation of professionals from a variety of fields (Barr et al., 1999), a rich diversity of knowledge and skills is available as a resource in the provision of health care (Loxley, 1997). In order to communicate effectively with health care recipients from diverse backgrounds and with other professionals, interprofessional collaboration involving advanced relationship skills is essential (Tresolini et al., 1994).

The preparation of health professionals has been identified as a key way of achieving collaborative practice (Brandon and Knapp, 1999; Clark, 1997; Glen, 1996; World Health Organisation (WHO), 1988). Various approaches to the preparation of health professionals have been used (Alsop and Vigars, 1998). Shared learning entails the maintenance of distinct educational programs, with students from different professions jointly addressing common curriculum content. Joint training involves the provision of one educational program with a core curriculum that addresses common content and with courses that focus on discipline-specific issues. Dual qualification integrates the learning requirements of two professions within one program, providing qualifications in both professions. Interprofessional education, sometimes referred to as multiprofessional education, is:

> a process by which a group of students from the health-related occupations with different educational backgrounds learn together during certain periods of their education, with interaction as an important goal, to collaborate in providing promotive, preventive, curative, rehabilitative and other health-related services (WHO, 1988, pp. 6–7).

The distinctive feature of interprofessional education, as noted by Alsop and Vigars (1998), is its focus on the development of skills for interacting with members of other professions. If, as Clark (1997) argues, professions have their own unique systems of meaning, the essence of interprofessional education is learning to communicate across cultures.

By definition, interprofessional education involves at least two professions, but often includes several. A variety of institutional arrangements exist (Brandon and Knapp, 1999). Approaches range from creating distinct units that provide interprofessional education, to infusing content regarding collaboration into the curricula of several professions. Instruction may be at either the undergraduate or graduate level and may be either mandatory or elective. The amount of content can be limited to the inclusion of one module within an existing course or as extensive as the provision of a sequence of courses. Numerous descriptions of interprofessional education are found in the literature (Banks and Janke, 1998; Barr et al., 1999; Betz, and Turman, 1997; Browne et al., 1995; Carpenter, 1995; Kristjanson et al., 1997; Parsell and Bligh, 1998; Richardson et al., 1999; Rudman, Ward and Varekojis, 1999; Russell and Hymans, 1999).

Overview of the Course

The interprofessional course we have developed is a four-week intensive course that prepares senior students in the health professions to respond effectively as individuals and members of a team to the HIV/AIDS epidemic and its consequences, both biological and social. Knowledge, values and abilities required for interprofessional and discipline-specific work are addressed with an emphasis on beginning the development of skills to work in partnership with people living with HIV/AIDS, their families and friends, and community agencies. The course is designed to be offered to six students from each of medicine, pharmaceutical sciences, nursing and social work. Over the four years that we have offered the course, various constellations of faculty members and students have participated. In 1997, medicine, nursing and pharmacy students were involved in a pilot course. In 1998, medical students were unable to attend due to scheduling problems while social work students joined with students from nursing and pharmaceutical sciences. In 1999 and 2000, students from all four professions participated. The course is unique in that it addresses interprofessional education with a sole focus on a particular disease and includes both discipline-specific as well as interdisciplinary content and practice.

Rationale

One reason for providing interprofessional education in relation to HIV/AIDS prevention and care is that effective intervention with respect to this chronic, complex, infectious disease requires collaboration among an array of professionals, community members and people with HIV/AIDS (PWAs). Considerable expertise in HIV/AIDS prevention and care is centred in Vancouver, in part because the city has the unfortunate distinction of having one of the highest incidences of the disease in Canada. Consequently, excellent resources are available for teaching and learning. At the University of British Columbia the development of the elective was supported by three factors: the Faculty of Medicine was involved in a curriculum revision project emphasising its commitment to responding to its societal obligations, the School of Nursing had experience in offering an HIV/AIDS care elective in collaboration with the British Columbia Centre for Excellence in HIV/AIDS and AIDS service and advocacy organisations, and the Office of the Coordinator of Health Sciences was revitalising interprofessional education. The availability of funding from the National HIV/AIDS Strategy of Health Canada for the development of interprofessional education supported our focus on this particular disease.

The Evolving Model

Models of interprofessional education that guide development of curricula and individual courses are not articulated clearly. In Canada, the United States and the United Kingdom, interprofessional education initiatives tend to be tailored to the particular requirements and resources of the setting (Barr et al., 1999; Loxley, 1997). Gelmon (1996) and Betz and Turman (1997) have identified the need to articulate competencies and standards for interprofessional education. Also, Barr et al. (1999) have recognised the need to develop a typology of interprofessional education before answers can be sought about its outcomes. Gelmon (1996) has raised questions about the relationship between educational accreditation and interprofessional learning in the health professions and indicated that models may be helpful in the process of developing competencies and setting standards. Loxley (1997, p. 69) has argued that 'Interprofessional education needs a conceptual framework against which it can assess itself, and against which it can be measured, to justify and resource it'. The model evolving from our experiences with interprofessional education is a response to this need and has three interrelated elements: partnership, collaborative process and course design.

Partnership

Partnerships are essential to the provision of classroom and clinical learning experiences in interprofessional education and to succeed, require that ways of working together be delineated. Our partnerships are with individuals from three interrelated areas: 1) health and social service professionals in practice; 2) professionals teaching in health and social service disciplines at the University; and 3) PWAs and/or people working in HIV/AIDS advocacy and support organisations. A core-working group, composed of individuals representing each of the three partner areas, is responsible for the delivery of the course. This group emerged from a larger planning committee when it became evident that collaboration among a smaller number of individuals, who were committed to interprofessional education and able to dedicate time to it, was required if the project was to succeed.

Collaborative Process

A central component of the model is the collaborative process. The key phases of this process are assessing, building, managing and evaluating (Loxley, 1997). Recognition of these phases came through reflection on the course planning meetings, experiences teaching the course and review of the literature. In the intensive and lengthy course meetings, faculty struggled to state the objectives for the course, develop a framework to organise the varied content and identify the teaching and learning experiences.

Assessing

One facet of this phase is identifying education needs as perceived by faculty, practitioners, those infected and affected by the disease and students. Another facet is determining teacher, practice, and institutional expertise, support and resources. Finally, appraisal of enabling structures is essential and is linked to consideration of funding sources, institutional support and resources. In our experience, the process of examining these issues reveals information about the culture and values of group members, the influence of power on relationships among group members and the flexibility of professional boundaries.

Building

In this phase, the course design is developed and working relationships that enable the collaborative process are established. Another activity is dealing with known barriers in the system; for example, the difficulty of finding a time to offer the course given the varied and complex course scheduling in each faculty.

The structure for collaboration emerges as working relationships are established. The culture and values of the group become known and boundaries are established that give the group identity (Loxley, 1997). Respect for differences in values, beliefs and expertise is essential to effective collaboration for interprofessional teaching (Glen, 1999). Power issues must be acknowledged and dealt with as they occur and recur. In our course design process, deciding about the interprofessional objectives and learning experiences required us to work with these differences (Loxley, 1997). This process resulted in the establishment of trust and group identity. It helped us understand the skills and abilities of each group member and build a way of working together.

The quality of relationships among members of the teaching team affects the worth of interprofessional education (Tresolini et al., 1994). Knowledge, skills and values for practitioner–practitioner relationships have been developed using the areas of self-awareness, traditions of knowledge in the health professions, building teams and communities and working dynamics of teams, groups and organisations. Examination of these ideas is part of our ongoing consideration of ways to strengthen the working relationship aspect of the building phase.

Managing

The delivery of the course is the focus of this phase. Both the interprofessional teaching team and the students work to achieve the desired course outcomes. Approaches to maintain and foster the working relationships established in the building phase and to deal with conflict need to be identified and applied. Interchange of information about all aspects of the learning experiences must flourish if collaborative teaching and learning is to be successful.

In our experience, designating one member of the teaching team as the leader for each class day promotes both organisation and communication. Whether or not all of the teaching team members need to be present for all classes is open to question. The course is an intensive one, taught over a four-week period, and this design characteristic influences the management phase. The intensity of the course appears to promote the collaborative process.

In our model, managing the collaborative process involves relating with students who are also managing their own work in student interprofessional teams. Language is an aspect that is particularly helpful to consider. Collaboration requires developing an understanding of the meanings of words and use of terms in the various professions (Loxley, 1997). To succeed, both teachers and students from different disciplines should seek feedback about communication so that ambiguity can be reduced and interactions enriched.

Evaluating

The outcomes of collaboration must be determined. Have the educational objectives been achieved? What are the perspectives of the teaching team, students, practitioners in clinical settings, guest lecturers, PWAs? Approaches to evaluating the outcomes of interprofessional education in terms of the collaborative process are not well developed. The first steps in delineating these approaches may be to develop the theory base for collaboration (Loxley, 1997), to articulate competencies, standards and models for interprofessional education.

Course Design

A third component of the interprofessional education model, the course design, emerges during the building phase of the collaborative process. Our course is built around discipline-specific and interprofessional learning in the context of HIV/AIDS. The main organising foci are teaching and learning about interprofessional work and teaching and learning about HIV/AIDS. Themes regarding diversity are woven around these two foci.

Two elements of the course that relate to both the discipline-specific and interprofessional learning experiences are care of self and reflection. Learning experiences in these areas are included to ensure that students are supported during their exploration of sometimes difficult and challenging concepts and values, and during practice in care delivery situations characterised by diversity. Because burnout can be a significant concern in working with marginalised populations and interprofessional teams, helping students gain skills in caring for self while they care for others is an important aspect of the course.

Interprofessional Learning

Teaching and learning experiences help the students to achieve the course objectives with respect to interprofessional practice. First, knowledge, abilities and skills required to work with other professionals and in teams are explored. Second, interprofessional perspectives on HIV/AIDS prevention and care, particularly the social context of living with HIV/AIDS, are examined. Topics considered include sexuality, poverty, discrimination, drug use, and the psychosocial and spiritual aspects of care. Students are assigned to teams on the first day of class and learn in these teams during the course. Each team has one student from each of the disciplines of medicine, nursing, pharmaceutical sciences and social work.

Case-based learning is used to promote students' abilities to work as inter-professional team members. An example is the case of AB, a 30-year-old, gay, white, middle class male admitted to the palliative care unit for symptom management. This case offers students the opportunity to explore inter-professional work in a context where they usually have some knowledge and experience and where the role models for teamwork are excellent. AB represents an important group of individuals with HIV/AIDS and his middle class status means he, his partner and family have access to resources and are articulate participants in care decisions. The case is used to help student teams examine:

1 interprofessional team structure and function: exploring roles, professional capabilities and professional responsibilities;
2 planning and implementing collaborative care plans: thinking about team communication and sharing responsibilities to meet initial treatment goals;
3 resolving team conflict: discussing issues and roles around difficulty with decision-making and resolving team conflict;
4 managing ongoing conflict/crisis: discussing issues around ethics, such as those related to confidentiality and developing a strategy for managing team discord.

Two clinical learning experiences are directly related to the interprofessional objectives. Each student spends about four hours with a member of another discipline. For example, a medical student spends a morning with one of the home care nurses visiting clients in the inner city area with the highest incidence of HIV/AIDS; a nursing student spends time with a physician on the AIDS care unit in a teaching hospital; a pharmacy student spends time with the nurse in a day care centre for PWAs and a social work student spends time with the pharmacist who specialises in drug therapy for PWAs. For the second experience, each student team observes a meeting of an interprofessional practice team caring for PWAs in a hospital or community setting.

Meeting with PWAs in student interprofessional teams is a significant experience that occurs in the first week of the course. It helps students to understand what it is like to live with HIV/AIDS and to begin to understand lifestyles different from their own. In addition, the experience appears to help students appreciate the values and attitudes they share across professional and personal boundaries.

For one of the course assignments, students present as an interprofessional team. The assignment is designed to help students: a) develop their knowledge of opportunistic infections and intervention strategies used to promote health; and b) increase their ability to work in an interprofessional group and to present material from an interprofessional perspective. This assignment is a source of both tension and enjoyment for the students. Each of them must become knowledgeable about an opportunistic infection and therapy/care provided by his/her own discipline. At the same time, each student must work collaboratively with his/her team members to present material from an interprofessional point of view.

Discipline-specific Learning

The teaching and learning experiences about discipline-specific work occur mainly in clinical practice settings and are designed to help the students achieve the course objectives with respect to HIV/AIDS. During their discipline-specific clinical experiences, students work with health professionals who model effective practice and frequently act as mentors. Experiences in hospital and community settings are provided. The nature of the clinical experiences varies from discipline to discipline. One written assignment has both a discipline-specific element and an interprofessional element.

Evidence of Effectiveness of the Model

The course has been evaluated in various ways and each year the students have rated the course experience highly. The pilot course was assessed using a multidimensional evaluation design (Trussler et al., 1998). Reflective sessions, a major part of this evaluation, were used to learn about the impact of the course on students' attitudes from week to week. Analysis of qualitative data gathered during these sessions provided evidence that the course impacted on students' self-awareness, conceptions of practice and skills in interprofessional teamwork. A significant insight was that the power and intensity of students' experiences linked to HIV and the conditions in which it flourishes pushed students to transcend professional boundaries and enabled them to realise the value of interprofessional work.

The evaluation also suggested that guided reflective sessions can contribute to interprofessional learning and practice. However, in relation to course evaluation, Trussler et al. (1998, p. 26) found:

> Interprofessionalism as a topic was difficult territory to interrogate too directly in these sessions. Although discussions opened up occasionally, the subject was hardly a hot-button and more or less taken-for-granted. Nevertheless, the reflective sessions in themselves were interprofessional events and as such worth examining for their group dynamics.

In the two subsequent offerings of the course, it was difficult to achieve effective discussion of interprofessional issues during the reflective sessions. The reasons for this difficulty are unclear but the skill of the facilitator and students' comfort with reflection on practice are two factors that need to be examined further.

The impact of interprofessional education on health outcomes is a significant area that requires examination. The lack of attention to this area (Barr et al., 1999) is in part due to the challenges inherent in trying to control for the array of factors which intervene between the training of professionals and the delivery of services. In our evaluation of the course to date, we have not addressed this key aspect of the evaluation.

Strengths of the Model

In our experience, a particular strength of this model of interprofessional education is that the course provides for both discipline-specific and interprofessional learning. A benefit of this more complex design is that it addresses one of the criticisms of interprofessional education – that it can contribute to blurring professional boundaries and impede the development of professional identities (Lindeke and Block, 1998). In this model, students have the opportunity to clarify roles through classroom presentations as well as cross-disciplinary and interdisciplinary clinical experiences. In addition, as students interpret to others what their roles are, and as they participate with members of their own discipline in clinical experiences, they may strengthen their professional identities.

The focus on a disease that in North America disproportionately affects populations marginalised by virtue of poverty, ethnicity, sexual orientation and intravenous drug use, resulted in diversity emerging as a pivotal theme in this model of interprofessional education. The formation of partnerships with service recipients, community agencies, and health and social service practitioners in teaching about HIV/AIDS care provided rich learning opportunities. Students were able to learn directly from service recipients, many of whom had values and experiences distinct from their own, about the manifold meanings of illness and perceptions regarding health care. Because of the multiple service needs of PWAs, students also encountered a wide range of care providers with different values, skills and experiences. From people working in agencies, students could learn about community support systems and their limitations. Health and social service practitioners could help students understand the unique contributions their professions make to intervention in relation to a complex disease and demonstrate how they collaborate with each other. Thus students experienced the cultural complexity and professional challenges that many health care providers confront every day in practice.

Challenges in Collaborating

During the collaborative process, we encountered logistical, pedagogical and institutional challenges. Logistically, it is preferable to have roughly equal numbers of students from each participating profession in interprofessional courses. However, consistent with others' experiences, differences in scheduling in various professional faculties and schools present barriers to participation for many students. To maximise accessibility, the course is taught in a concentrated four-week block in June.

A second challenge that has both practical and pedagogical aspects is the difficulty in finding clinical placements. In part this challenge is mitigated by the fact that the core faculty are drawn from each of the four professions involved in the course. These faculty members arrange opportunities for same-profession, cross-profession, and interprofessional team experiences. Collaboration and teamwork often occur spontaneously in informal encounters that students may not recognise as interprofessional practice. Therefore, it is important to choose professionals who are able to articulate to students the dynamics that are occurring in their practice. Achieving this objective takes careful orientation of these clinical instructors, an ideal difficult to implement given the limited time practitioners have available.

Another pedagogical challenge is related to differences among students with respect to the knowledge they bring to the course, their motivations for taking the course and their preferred learning styles. We have addressed knowledge differences by having students who are already familiar with content in a particular area, present to their peers. With respect to motivations, some students are mainly interested in learning about HIV/AIDS prevention and care rather than about interprofessional collaboration. Therefore, we have emphasised in the recruitment of students that learning about interprofessional practice is a primary goal of the course. Finally, students' comfort with various educational approaches varies. Our model attempts to address these differences by utilising an array of teaching methods ranging from presentations by experts in various fields to group presentations by students regarding case examples.

The most significant institutional challenge we have encountered is accessing resources. The course is expensive in that it involves one faculty member from each profession in addition to community partners in planning, organising and delivering the course. Because of the need to provide clinical experiences for each student, we have had to limit the number of students each year to twenty-four. In part these costs have been absorbed by the various educational units and by fund raising from private sources.

Reflections and Questions

Our experience raises a number of questions in relation to the model. We recognise that aspects of learning about interprofessional practice in terms of values, knowledge and skills are integrated throughout the course. However, we wonder whether, on balance, the focus on HIV/AIDS, with all its connotations of urgency and diversity, detracts from achieving the inter-professional learning objectives of the course. How effective would the model be if the course focused on other health issues, for instance, provision of care for older people, people with disabilities, or people with addictions? We also realise that we have only begun to evaluate the model in terms of its processes and outcomes. For instance, we do not understand the motivations of the students in deciding to take the course. Although the course is an elective, some students may choose to take it primarily because of scheduling or primarily because of their learning goals with respect to HIV/AIDS. How many professions can effectively be involved in an interprofessional course? What are the changes in knowledge, values and skills that occur as a result of the course? Does the fact that students work together during the course mean that they are actually developing skills? Will the changes be transferable to practice and endure in various settings over time?

We realise that our model needs further development and evaluation. However, it does identify an ideal to strive towards in professional education

– to facilitate effective interprofessional collaboration. In organising and presenting this course, we have found that the professions involved shared a deep commitment to enhancing the well being of service recipients. The challenge will be to bring about changes in the structures of professional education so that the resources to effectively provide interprofessional education and care can be brought together.

Acknowledgements

The authors would like to acknowledge financial support from the National HIV/AIDS Strategy of Health Canada and the British Columbia Medical Services Foundation. This interprofessional course is one of six sponsored by the Office of the Coordinator of Health Sciences of the University of British Columbia.

References

Almgren, G. (1998), 'Mental Health Practice in Primary Care: Some Perspectives Concerning the Future of Social Work in Organized Delivery Systems', *Smith College Studies in Social Work*, 68 (2), pp. 233–53.
Alsop, A. and Vigars, C. (1998), 'Shared Learning, Joint Training or Dual Qualification in Occupational Therapy and Social Work: A feasibility study', *British Journal of Occupational Therapy*, 61 (4), pp. 146–52.
Banks, S. and Janke, K. (1998), 'Developing and Implementing Interprofessional Learning in a Faculty of Health Professions', *Journal of Allied Health*, 27 (3), pp. 132–6.
Barr, H., Hammick, M., Koppel, I. and Reeves, S. (1999), 'Systematic Review of the Effectiveness of Interprofessional Education: Towards transatlantic collaboration', *Journal of Allied Health*, 28 (2), pp. 104–8.
Betz, C.L. and Turman, J. (1997), 'A Process of Developing Terminal Competencies for an Interdisciplinary Training Program', *Journal of Allied Health*, 26 (3), pp. 113–18.
Brandon, R.N. and Knapp, M.S. (1999), 'Interprofessional Education and Training: Transforming Professional Preparation to Transform Human Services', *American Behavioral Scientist*, 42 (5), pp. 876–91.
Browne, A, Carpenter, C., Cooledge, C., Drover, G., Ericksen, J., Fielding, D., Hill, D., Johnston, J., Segal, S., Silver, J. and Sweeney, V. (1995), 'Bridging the Professions: An integrated and interdisciplinary approach to teaching health care ethics', *Academic Medicine*, 70 (11), pp. 1002–5.
Carpenter, J. (1995), 'Interprofessional Education for Medical and Nursing Students: Evaluation of a programme', *Medical Education*, 29 (4), pp. 265–72.
Clark, P.G. (1997), 'Values in Health Care Professional Socialization: Implications for geriatric education in interdisciplinary teamwork', *The Gerontologist*, 37 (4), pp. 441–51.

Gelmon, S.B. (1996), 'Can Educational Accreditation Drive Interdisciplinary Learning in the Health Professions?', *Journal of Quality Improvement*, 22 (3), pp. 213–22.

Glen, S. (1999), 'Educating for Interprofessional Collaboration: Teaching about values', *Nursing Ethics*, 6 (3), pp. 202–13.

Green, J.W. (1999), *Cultural Awareness in the Human Services: A multi-ethnic approach*, Allyn and Bacon, Needham Heights, Mass.

Kristjanson, L., Dudgeon, D., Nelson, F., Henteleff, P. and Balneaves, L. (1997), 'Evaluation of an Interdisciplinary Training Program in Palliative Care: Addressing the needs of rural and northern communities', *Journal of Palliative Care*, 13 (3), pp. 5–12.

Lavizzo-Mourey, R.J. and MacKenzie, W. (1995), 'Cultural Competence – An Essential Hybrid for Delivering High Quality Care in the 1990s and Beyond', *Transactions of the American Clinical and Climatological Association*, 107, pp. 226–37.

Lindeke, L.L. and Block, D.E. (1998), 'Maintaining Professional Integrity in the Midst of Interdisciplinary Collaboration', *Nursing Outlook*, 46 (5), pp. 213–18.

Loxley, A. (1997), *Collaboration in Health and Welfare: Working with difference*, Jessical Kingsley, London.

Owen, J.W. (1998), 'Interprofessional Education and the Impact of the New White and Green Papers: A Health Perspective', paper presented at the Centre for the Advancement of Interprofessional Education, 17 June, London.

Parsell, G. and Bligh, J. (1998), 'Interprofessional Learning', *Postgraduate Medical Journal*, 74, pp. 89–95.

Richardson, J., Montemuro, M., Mohide, E.A., Cripps, D. and Macpherson, A.S. (1999), 'Training for Interprofessional Teamwork – Evaluation of an Undergraduate Experience', *Educational Gerontology*, 25, pp. 411–34.

Rudman, S.V., Ward, K.M. and Varekojis, S.M. (1999), 'University-community Partnerships for Health: A model interdisciplinary service-learning project', *Journal of Allied Health*, 28 (2), pp. 109–12.

Russell, K.M. and Hymans, D. (1999), 'Interprofessional Education for Undergraduate Students', *Public Health Nursing*, 16 (4), pp. 254–62.

Tresolini, C.P. and the Pew-Fetzer Task Force on Advancing Psychosocial Health Education (1994), *Health Professions Education and Relationship-centered Care*, Pew Health Professions Commission, San Francisco.

Trussler, T., Chalmers, A., Goldstone, I., Granger, P., McKinnon, S., Page, G., Perchal, P. and Wyness, A. (1998), *'Why Can't all Classes Be like This?' Evaluation of an Interprofessional Elective in HIV/AIDS Care*, unpublished manuscript.

World Health Organisation (1988), *Learning Together to Work Together for Health*, Technical Report Series 769, Geneva.

Chapter Six

Getting the Message Across:
Mental Health Matters in Older Age

Terry Downes and Jayne Sayers

This chapter introduces a new concept in the identification and management of mental health problems in older people at primary care level. Throughout most of the twentieth century survival prospects have improved, mainly because of declines in infant mortality and increasingly due to reductions in mortality in late, middle and early old age that are increasing longevity. Over the last 17 years, the probability of a 50-year-old female surviving to 75 years has improved by 8 per cent and it is only in the last few years that a majority of 50-year-old men in the UK could expect to live to 75 years of age (Warnes, 1993).

Psychiatric epidemiological studies (Gurland et al., 1983) have shown that mental health problems are common in the elderly, especially depression and dementia, together with anxiety disorders and alcohol misuse. At present, it seems that many elderly people are not offered any treatment or support for their mental health problems. Primary health care workers need to be aware of the prevalence of mental health problems in the community, the risk factors associated with their development, and methods of detecting them, including questionnaire and interview instruments. Given increasing longevity, there is a growing need for primary care teams to organise their services between them in ways that help to ensure that psychological problems in older people are effectively detected and treated.

A review of mental health services for the elderly (Vora and Baker, 1998) carried out in South Birmingham by GP commissioning groups, highlighted the following concerns; a lack of awareness of specialist knowledge in mental health issues affecting older people, excessive case loads carried by community psychiatric nurses and a lack of support from specialist services.

Studies have suggested that, on average, GP's identify only around half of the psychological problems among the patients presenting to them (Marks

Organisation Development in Health Care: Strategic Issues in Health Care Management, R.K. Rushmer, H.T.O. Davies, M. Tavakoli and M. Malek (eds), Ashgate Publishing Ltd, 2002.

et al., 1979). Many patients present with physical rather than psychological complaints and psychiatric problems associated with physical disease are less likely to be acknowledged as needing treatment in their own right. This is likely to be more of a problem with elderly than with younger patients, since the prevalence of physical disorders rises with age.

To address some of the problems identified locally, South Birmingham Mental Health NHS Trust Older Adult Directorate took an innovative approach in July 1998 by developing a service which aims to raise the profile of mental health in older people at primary care level. The closure of a continuing care unit gave the opportunity to reinvest, strengthening community services for older people with mental health problems, hence the Primary Care Liaison service was introduced. Five 'G' grade nurses were appointed to work in South Birmingham's five primary care groups. The nurses designated for this role are attached to general practices and work with GPs and their teams to assist in the early recognition, diagnosis and appropriate treatment of mental health problems in elderly people. The six objectives of the Primary Care Liaison service will now be discussed in detail.

Assessment

The aim of this facet of the role is to provide GPs and other members of the primary health care team with a greater understanding and awareness of the mental health needs of individual patients. The liaison nurse is available to GPs to conduct formal nursing based mental health assessments to determine the presence or absence of mental health problems in older people, subject to certain criteria. As the service operates at primary care level, any patient that is referred for assessment should be non urgent and not at risk and any individual deemed to be at risk should be referred to specialist secondary mental health services via existing channels. In addition, the liaison nurse is available to carry out informal mental health assessments where the need for a more flexible approach is identified. District nurses have often requested joint home visits and this has become a popular approach.

Training

The rapid increase in the number of employed practice nurses has increased the potential for teamwork in the care of mental ill health in general practice.

There is, however, little evidence that practice nurses are involved at all in the management of psychiatric problems, except in a few cases where they administer depot injections. Tudor-Hart (1985) has pointed out that they are an under-used resource and could be a valuable help if trained properly, given enough time, and allowed to maintain skills by continued experience. The annual routine screening of patients over the age of 75 has been in operation since 1990. Practice nurses are usually instrumental in carrying this out and it has been suggested that such screening should include questions to detect probable depression and dementia and to assess social networks (Illiffe et al., 1991).

General practitioners may also be unaware of the development of dementia in some of their patients. Iliffe et al. found a diagnosis of dementia recorded in the GP notes in only one of the 11 cases which they found on screening elderly people in north London with the mini mental state examination.

Therefore, the remit of the training component of the role is to enhance the level of knowledge and understanding about mental health in older people. The liaison service offers informal and formal training to every member of the primary health care team, which is planned to reflect the needs of individuals and groups on a wide range of mental health issues. The training also aims to explore attitudes and beliefs about mental illness and well-being in older age and discuss how these attitudes and beliefs may affect current practice. Thus, the training enables primary health care teams to apply theory to practice in a meaningful way, thereby enhancing skills to meet the mental health needs of their patients.

As a new and developing service, it is important that the evolving liaison role is monitored and evaluated for the impact that it has on primary and secondary care. To date, the training facet of the role has been evaluated in order to elicit what recipients thought of the training they received, including how relevant and useful they felt the information was and how far it met individual needs. A variety of different primary health care staff have received training including community care coordinators, district nurses, practice nurses, volunteers, coordinators and GPs. Topics have included the importance of differential diagnosis, dementia, depression, sleep disturbance in mental health, bereavement and the use of living wills and advance directives.

Mental Health Promotion

Promoting positive mental health is one of the greatest challenges facing western societies. Mental health really does matter. It matters to individuals, to groups of people in families, networks and communities. Critically understanding the ways that older people experience mental distress and the ways that others have viewed them provides insights that can contribute to better promotion of mental health in the future.

The service, therefore, aims to promote and maintain positive mental health in older people by providing information in various forms, all of which emphasise the importance of recognising and maintaining mental well-being. The service actively participates in national campaigns that positively promote the importance of mental health and seeks ways of challenging negative attitudes towards mental health in older people by replacing them with more positive images. The team had considerable input into local communities during Alzheimer's Awareness Week and World Mental Health Day in 1999 and was actively involved in contributing to the Millennium Carers' celebration in Birmingham during the summer of 2000.

Networking

Another key aim of the role is to promote collaborative working at primary care level to enable the health and social care needs of local people to be addressed in a more holistic way. Therefore, each liaison nurse began by identifying the various health and social care agencies that can contribute positively to holistic care within each primary care group, the rationale being to exchange ideas and information with the overall intention of increasing levels of knowledge and understanding about the valuable contribution that each organisation can make.

This has enabled various disciplines to identify existing barriers and to work collaboratively and seek to identify ways of over coming these in the quest to develop a seamless service. In two Primary Care Groups in South Birmingham, a variety of disciplines have come together to work with their respective liaison nurse to develop a screening tool for older people which aims to assess thoroughly, not only physical and social needs but also cognitive and emotional well-being.

Each liaison nurse has extensively researched their respective primary care group in order to compile a South Birmingham resource directory to provide information about services available to older people and their carers. This directory is evaluated on an ongoing basis and is available to the primary health care team.

Audit and Quality

The team is able to offer primary health care teams the opportunity to access various audit and quality projects. This aspect of the role enables the liaison nurse to describe and promote the benefits of audit and evaluation in relation to improving the quality of mental health care in line with clinical governance. By identifying desired standards of practice that are specific, measurable, achievable, realistic and within agreed time limits, primary health care teams can make informed judgements whether previously identified standards are being achieved. One such example is the audit of antidepressant medication in relation to compliance in older people. Wilkinson et al. (1993) found that practice nurses could assist GPs in the management of depression, by advising patients about potential side effects of antidepressants in an effort to increase compliance with treatment.

Advice and Support

The primary care of mental illness in older people should be more efficient and effective where other members of the primary care team besides the GP are involved, including district nurses, health visitors and practice nurses. These professionals are in frequent contact with many patients and could assist the GP in preventing, identifying and managing mental illness in primary care. Therefore, the liaison nurses are accessible to primary health care teams, to provide evidence-based information about mental health; thereby enabling them to make informed choices about mental health issues specific to individual patients and carers.

Progress

This chapter will now discuss a variety of projects that have been undertaken over the 12 months preceding the time of writing that have enabled the service to work collaboratively with primary health care teams and other agencies in order to challenge ageist assumptions in order to effect change.

Over the past 10 years, there have been huge advances in the range of services available at primary care level, including asthma and diabetic clinics that have helped to facilitate patient care. For the first time, practice attached liaison nurses have made it possible for the development of practice registers of vulnerable, elderly people with mental health needs. This has enabled more proactive and preventative management of such patients. The service has been able to offer practices the opportunity to hold 'healthy ageing' days where all patients over the age of 75 are invited to attend the surgery on a specific day during October/November for a flu vaccination, chiropody appointment and B/P monitoring with the practice nurse. This is followed by a discussion with the liaison nurse that specifically addresses the older person's psychological well-being, enabling problems to be flagged up and discussed with the individual patient. Also in attendance on these days are representatives from Age Concern and social services who have proven to be a very valuable source of information to older people and their carers.

The liaison service has also offered practices the opportunity to set up carers' registers for carers looking after older people with mental health problems. By asking carers to identify themselves to the practice receptionist, the liaison nurse is able to set up a register and hold regular 'carer forums' where carers can gain information about services that will aid their caring role. During many of these sessions, the liaison nurses have often identified carer distress and have been able to work with the carer in order to refer the individual carer to the most appropriate source of help. This has been instrumental in helping to eliminate the potential for another mental health problem existing within the same family as it is often when the carer reaches crisis point that the person they are caring for is admitted to secondary care.

Practice nurses in some surgeries have requested liaison nurses to initiate clinical pathways for detecting and managing certain mental health problems in older people. Depression is the most commonly asked for clinical pathway and this is currently being used in various practices across all five primary care groups in south Birmingham.

The liaison nurses have also been able to influence the face of mental illness in older people in a variety of ways by becoming actively involved in various projects and steering groups across South Birmingham. Examples of such involvement include representation on Health Improvement Steering groups within primary care groups and participation in the Regional Mental Health Promotion Steering Group.

Proposed Future Developments

Through the various aspects of the role, liaison nurses have much contact with patients. 'How is it then that despite statements by Health and Local

Authorities that they consult users, older people who use mental health services still feel that they have little or no control over most service planning or provision?' Most government directives explicitly specify that local purchasers and providers should consult with service users. However, there is often a substantial gap between these good intentions and outcomes that are satisfactory to individual patients. Via the process of assessment, the liaison nurses then discuss individual need with patients and make specific recommendations to the GP. Overwhelmingly, patients are often identified as requiring and indeed request, a befriending service. In South Birmingham this resource is sadly lacking and the liaison service has built into the evaluation process the provision to flag up unmet need. This is an attempt by the service to bridge the gap, by focusing on older people and what they want by considering ways in which they might be more effectively involved in the planning and running of services. Thus, there are now plans to work collaboratively with local agencies to initiate a befriending project for older people with mental health problems in South Birmingham in the not too distant future.

To conclude, it is necessary to discuss where the service is to date. The Primary Care Liaison service has now been operational for a year and during this time many primary health care staff have accessed the service, tapping into many different facets of the role according to the needs of the individual practice.

Referrals to the service for assessment, although slow to begin with, are now rapidly gaining momentum, which enables older people with mental health needs to be cared for at primary care level where appropriate. Through advice and support, the liaison service has helped to facilitate referrals to secondary care where the need has arisen, ensuring that older people gain access to the most appropriate service from the onset. Overwhelmingly, the most accessed facet of the role, at the present time, across all five primary care groups is the training component with requests for different sessions growing continually.

The role of the liaison nurse continues to evolve daily, taking on board suggestions and comments from primary health care teams in order to provide a needs led service. Primary care liaison has come along way since its inception and through its innovative approach of 'getting the message across, mental health matters in older age', working practices are being changed. Indeed, other areas of the country have expressed interest in setting up a similar initiative and the team were invited to East London last year and gave a presentation about the benefits of primary care liaison. Although still early days for a developing service, it would appear that South Birmingham's Primary Care Liaison service has become a valuable resource that has placed the needs of older people with mental health problems firmly on the agenda at primary care level.

References

Gurland, B., Copeland, J. and Kuriansky, J. et al. (1983), *The Mind and Mood of Ageing*, Croom Helm, London.

Illiffe, S., Haines, A., Gallivan, S. et al. (1991), 'Assessment of Elderly People in General Practice, Part 1: Social circumstances and mental state', *British Journal of General Practice*, 41, pp. 9–12.

Marks, J.N., Goldberg, G.P. and Hillier, V.F. (1979), 'Determinance of the Ability of General Practitioners to Detect a Psychiatric illness', *Psychological Medicine*, 9, pp. 337–53.

Tudor-Hart, J. (1985), 'Practice Nurses: An under used resource', *British Medical Journal*, 290, pp. 1162–3.

Vora, A. and Baker, P. (1998), unpublished work on mental health needs in the elderly by the Northfield and Kings Heath GP Commissioning Group, Birmingham.

Warnes, A.M. (1993), *The Demography of Ageing in the United Kingdom of Great Britain and Northern Ireland*, Committee for International Co-operation in National Research in Demography and the United Nations Institute on Ageing, Valletta, Malta.

Wilkinson, G., Allen, P. and Marshall, E. et al. (1993), 'The Role of the Practice Nurse in the Management of Depression in General Practice: Treatment adherence to anti-depressant medication', *Psychological Medicine*, 23, pp. 229–37.

SECTION THREE
LEADERSHIP

Chapter Seven

Primary Care Groups:
A Study into the Development of
Appropriate Managerial Skills

Helen Bussell, Lisa Cunnington, Carol Hornsby, Dorothy Noble
and Lisa Sinclair

Introduction

Primary Care Groups were established as a managerial board of health professionals in England and Wales (DoH, 1997) and started operating in shadow form at the end of October 1998. As Health Authority subcommittees they have been given devolved responsibility for the health care needs of their local community and are in a unique position to effect change. In order to carry out their role PCGs will require specific skills. It is envisaged that these skills will be acquired during the 'shadow' period (from October 1998 to April 1999) (Gilley, 1999).

PCGs may operate at one of four levels:

- level I; a PCG acts in support of the Health Authority in commissioning care for its population, acting in an advisory capacity;
- level II; it is still part of the Health Authority but takes responsibility for managing the budget for health care in their area;
- level III; the PCG is a freestanding body accountable to the Health Authority for commissioning care;
- level IV; it has the added responsibility for the provision of community services for their population.

PCGs which operate at level III or IV become Primary Care Trusts. However, it should be noted that, prior to 1 April 2000, PCGs have operated at levels I or II only (DoH, 2000).

Organisation Development in Health Care: Strategic Issues in Health Care Management, R.K. Rushmer, H.T.O. Davies, M. Tavakoli and M. Malek (eds), Ashgate Publishing Ltd, 2002.

To develop an understanding of the role and functions of the PCGs a project was commissioned by a Community Health Council (CHC) in North East England. The brief was to identify the training needs of Board members and to recommend an appropriate managerial training to develop those needs. This paper reports on the findings of this project and examines the managerial skills required of Board members to fulfil their role (as outlined by the Association of Community Health Councils in England and Wales (ACHC, 1998)) by investigating PCGs during their pilot period up to April 1999.

Methodology

The research was carried out during March and April 1999 while the PCG was operating in shadow form. As PCGs are a new organisation an exploratory investigation was considered to be the most appropriate

> to obtain some background information … to define problem areas fully … to identify relevant or salient behaviour patterns, beliefs, opinions, attitudes, motivations, etc. and to develop structures of these constructs (Malhotra and Birks, 1998, p. 78).

Given the exploratory nature of the research a case study approach was adopted based on the PCG within the CHC's boundary. This PCG was selected as it was of intrinsic interest (Stake, 1998) to the CHC and its members had agreed to participate fully in the research. A single case approach was deemed to be suitable as the individual members of the PCG provide 'subcases' (Yin, 1984) which allow for within-case analysis. Also 'the prime concern [was] with the conditions under which the construct or theory operates, not with the generalisation of the findings to other settings' (Miles and Huberman, 1994, p. 29).

Semi-structured in-depth interviews were carried out with all eleven PCG Board member. They were 'selected to participate in the research based on their first hand experience with a culture, social interaction and phenomenon of interest' (Streubert and Carpenter, 1995, p. 22). Each interview followed an interview schedule to gather data on the role and main functions of the PCG; the managerial skills, experience and formal qualifications of members and their views on future training needs; members' perceptions of key strategic issues. After transcription, the interview data was analysed using data reduction techniques (Strauss, 1987).

To provide a means of triangulation (Denzin, 1970) and to add breadth and depth to the investigation, questionnaires were distributed to three neighbouring PCGs. This was to obtain an overview of opinions and practices in the region and to provide a means of comparison. The questionnaire, based on data collected in the semi-structured interviews and secondary sources, covered the roles and functions of PCGs, managerial skills, strategic issues, areas of conflict and classification questions. After piloting it was mailed to 34 PCG members. Fourteen completed questionnaires were returned (41 per cent response rate) and analysed. Responses were received from each of the three neighbouring PCGs and each of the professional groups on PCG Boards was represented.

Findings – Case Study

Roles and Responsibilities

Apart from the lay person who applied for the post and was interviewed, Board members were nominated to be on the PCG. The Board was made up of seven GPs, two nursing representatives, one social services representative and one lay person. The Chief Executive had not yet been appointed.

When asked to outline the PCG's key tasks, the PCG's vision statement was cited as 'being an innovative, equitable organisation to determine and improve health and social care of patients and the public in the North East'. From this statement there were a number of areas which were identified as key tasks. First and foremost was the improvement of health. There was agreement that the key tasks are tied to the Health Improvement Programme and the four main areas identified by *Saving Lives, Our Healthier Nation* (DoH, 1988) (cancer, coronary heart disease, accidents, mental health) and Health Action Zones. In their initial set of priorities the Board also included issues such as diabetes, prescribing of antibiotics and teenage sexual health.

The Board's aim was to provide and maintain the best services possible for patients by working in partnership with other services. The role of the Board was in 'making sure that all these people working on their own mesh into the whole group and the broader plan' and they had set up formal mechanisms to develop collaborative working conditions, such as a number of subcommittees assigned to develop areas of clinical governance, commissioning and prescribing. There were also good links with the CHC, Social Services and the general public.

The importance of communication between the PCG and its key stakeholders was recognised. One member stressed that:

one of the principles of the PCG is to be open and accessible and we are looking at communication strategies which include open meetings, newsletters and specific people of the Board.

Reference was made to the 'multi-professional advisory group' initiated by the nursing members whereby representatives from all nursing disciplines maintain effective communication to feed information and opinions both down and up the communication channels. Another member stated 'We are consulting our constituents for everything we do ... We are working for them in a way. We are not working for ourselves.' This clearly showed that the Board intends to draw opinions from their stakeholders into their decision making.

The greatest problem identified was communication with the general public. The Board recognised that it needs to raise public awareness as many are unaware of the existence of PCGs. Monthly 'open' meetings are held but they have not been very effective in drawing in the public partly due to factors such as venues, timing and awareness (for example, they are not advertised prominently in the local media). Board members had also discussed how public relations issues would be handled until the Chief Executive was appointed and it had been agreed that this would be part of the Chair's role temporarily. Although some communications systems were in place it was felt that 'our PR is not as good as it could be'.

Although Board members recognised that conflicts of interest may occur from their decisions they were confident that they would be able to manage these situations. One member characterised the position as wearing a corporate hat and a practitioner hat and being able to divorce his day-to-day work from the PCG's strategic approach.

Conflicts between stakeholders were also recognised. As one member said 'the pie is only so big and you cannot cut it into enough slices'. The Board will have to assess the way budgets are distributed to key stakeholders and to ensure that services are provided most efficiently. This may cause conflict if funding is taken from one area and given to another with greater need.

The members unanimously believed that they worked well as a team. This may have been influenced by previous working relationships. The Board had a mutual respect for each other and made new members (i.e. those who were not part of previous working parties) feel comfortable and part of the team. One member felt that 'one of the reasons the PCG ... will work is because it does work very much, and has worked from the beginning, as a team'.

Some tension between the PCG and the Health Authority was apparent. The Board are aware that they are still 'only' a subcommittee of the Health Authority and there were suggestions that the Health Authority was hindering the progress of the PCG. Although this was improving there had been a need at times for the Board to be assertive. One member stated that 'There have been some interesting battles during the setting up process'.

Managerial Skills

The range of managerial skills identified as important were broad but there was much consensus across the Board. All felt that communication skills were vital as well as the ability to manage change effectively. 'It's all about change ultimately; to make it happen.' Other skills highlighted included budgetary control, leadership, managing meetings, managing people, negotiation skills, performance management. These were summarised by one member as 'overall good strategic management or clarity to strategic vision, commitment to change, managing people, managing money and communication are the key skills'.

It was clear that members did not feel they required team building skills. A number were aware of Belbin's work on teams (Harding and Long, 1998) and felt that the make-up of the Board was effective. 'Not everybody can do everything, but most people have something to offer'. It was accepted that some of the skills required were not universal, for example medical skills were not a prerequisite. A previous background of fund holding practice gave some members many of the skills necessary to perform their role on the Board. However, it was recognised that the varied backgrounds of members meant a variety of skills could be drawn upon and it was clear that members would ask for advice from fellow members and provide support.

Most accepted that although they were equipped to take on their new role, certain skills could be developed more. A typical view was: 'I see this as a development opportunity for me, but, Yes, I am as equipped as the next person.' Although a training package was being offered to all Board members by a local Business School, it became apparent that individual development was the key to improving members' skill requirements. Reference was also made to a variety of other training events and development opportunities. One member mentioned training offered by the Health Authority to explain to non-experts how the NHS works and how money flows around the organisation. When asked if the training offered met their needs a common response was: 'It does at the time. It depends on how much you put it into practice.' Board members felt somewhat overworked and so found there was insufficient time allowed to attend training courses.

The majority opinion when asked about managerial qualifications was 'No, but I have experience and time', although some members did have formal qualifications which included an element of management and many had management experience. 'There was a lot of management training went into fund holding when this started and a lot of managers and doctors did a lot of formal management training ... none of which gives you a degree.' The value of a management qualification was not acknowledged.

Strategic Issues

The main strength of the Board members was seen to be their knowledge of the local community and their ability to work well as a team as well as being 'dynamic and forward thinking and they're very geared towards being seen as fair and consultative and so very strong on the communication side'.

There was a general feeling that one of the greatest weaknesses was time management.

> I think the time scales people expect things to be produced in is inadequate ...
> Everyone is seeing patients and dealing with Social Service clients and so on
> and the PCG Board is fairly time consuming. But it doesn't mean that patients
> don't come through the door. So time is a constraining factor.

The lack of a support system for the Board is clearly an issue.

The main opportunity for the PCG Board was seen to be to improve the health care of the local community, to focus funding where it is required by directing services to those most in need and improve those areas receiving inadequate care at present. The centralisation of services locally could also improve quality.

There was concern that the PCG would be seen as, or become, another administrative layer in the NHS. Some members feared that there could be yet another restructuring in the future or that there were plans to merge PCGs. Some were anxious that a 'hidden agenda' on the part of government could pose a threat. Funding was regarded as a crucial issue. 'We may not get monies in order to meet the needs of the population.' One member questioned whether politicians were passing the responsibility of inadequate resources onto the PCGs. PCGs were seen as competing for a share of the funding from the 'central pot'.

There was a general consensus about why the PCG had started at level II. The GP members had been working at an equivalent to Level I for a number of years and, therefore, the Board saw level II as an opportunity to have the autonomy to be able to make the changes that they had only been able to advise on previously. Although all members wanted to see the PCG at level IV in 12 months time they certainly hoped to achieve level III. At the time of the interviews the legislation was being written for Trusts but 'we don't want to jump to Trust unless there are some tangible gains, we will look at the whole package closely'.

When asked what skills were needed to gain Trust status the first response of many members was that a Chief Executive was the first requirement before the PCG considers moving to a higher level. Members also identified once again those skills that they needed to enhance at present as those required for future development. The need for a clear infrastructure and communication strategy was also highlighted.

Members indicated that their measure of success would be to see that patients receive the best services and that these were distributed equitably. The presence of effective clinical governance systems was regarded as one measure of success against the targets set. One member suggested that a long-term measure of success would be whether the health of the nation measure for the area (based on mortality rates) had been reduced.

Findings – Comparative Study

Roles and Responsibilities

Unlike the case study PCG, just over one-third of those responding had been nominated for membership. Apart from the lay person and Chief Executive (who had been appointed through a selection process) the rest had referred themselves onto the Board. While suggesting a willingness by members to be part of the organisation this may not be the most effective way of recruiting the right people.

All the PCGs studied appeared to be working towards achieving the same goals. However, there was some confusion over which health areas should be prioritised as a wide range of key health areas were identified. Only two of the national targets, coronary heart disease and mental health, appeared high on these PCGs' agenda.

Inter-agency working was being developed through joint working on Health Action Zones (HAZ) and Health Improvement Programmes (HImP). Each PCG had established subgroups to develop collaborative working arrangements but not all relevant professional groups were always represented. The majority of responses expressed the need for a communication strategy and suggested this was in the process of being developed, although what was currently in place varied greatly.

Although working relationships with the Locality Teams of the Health Authority was good for all three PCGs, at the higher levels there were issues regarding support which appeared to be causing some friction between the Health Authority and the PCGs.

Respondents were asked to rate team working within their Board. All stressed that it was early days. Responses indicated that all members were committed, enthusiastic and highly motivated and that team working will develop over time. However, team working arrangements were not yet fully established in some Boards. Some were having problems in arranging Board meetings. Meetings were considered to be poorly chaired and tended not to run to time, resulting in increasing conflict between members.

Managerial Skills

The key managerial skills identified were similar to those highlighted by members of the case study PCG and indicate that there is a set of core managerial skills required by a PCG to perform key tasks. These include change management, commissioning, communication, decision making, financial skills, human resource management, leadership, strategic planning, team building, time management.

The majority of respondents (64 per cent) did not have any managerial qualifications and just over half (57 per cent) had received training/support for their new role. Responses indicated that past experience was often deemed to be sufficient, although respondents acknowledged that they did not have all the management skills necessary to perform their current role within the PCG. A number of areas were identified where further training was felt to be required.

Conflict Management

The main area identified for potential conflict was funding and competition for resources. It was also recognised that there may be some conflict on the part of GPs as a result of interest in their practice. It was felt that good team working and support would help to manage conflict efficiently and effectively. However, members had limited experience of managing conflict and had no public relations skills.

Strategic Issues

Respondents identified that the key professional groups were well represented on each Board. Members' expertise was seen to be a major strength for future development but lack of time and resources could hinder this development if not addressed.

Respondents agreed with the case study PCG regarding the opportunities available and the threats to PCGs. A recent merger of two neighbouring Hospital Trusts led to concern about future mergers of PCGs, particularly as one PCG had chosen to start at level I due to lack of previous fund holding experience. Half the respondents thought that their PCG would gain Trust status some time in the future but did not know when. None thought that this would be achieved within the next 12 months. The majority believed that their PCG would continue operating at level II. In order to gain Trust status it was felt that management skills and a sound management structure with firm control over budgets would have to be developed as well as collaborative working arrangements to ensure stakeholder support.

As with the case study PCG, the main indicator for success was seen to be the development of primary care service for the population area. However, others, often linked to skills development, were identified

Conclusion

All interviewees displayed a high level of commitment and appeared to have met the very demanding time scales placed upon them. Although members were obviously enthusiastic and optimistic in facing the challenges presented to them, there is a danger that the pace of organisational change required and the continued commitment needed may detract from the process. Members recognised the importance of enhancing existing managerial skills and how these were to be applied effectively to their level of functional responsibility to successfully influence outcomes.

During the study it became apparent that the selected PCG was not typical in terms of its organisation and skills and in fact presented an example of best practice. This was confirmed by the Chief Executive of a local business school, which had been assessing the PCG through observation. He concluded that:

> the ... PCG Board is not typical of all PCG Boards. Their past experiences and working practices have equipped them with many of the managerial skills required to undertake this new venture.

For example, the case study PCG had clearly recognised the importance of prioritising key health areas, unlike the neighbouring PCGs who had some obvious difficulty with prioritisation. All PCGs in the study considered that an effective communication system was vital as a means to achieving its objectives but the case study PCG had progressed further than others in the region in developing this. Team-working was also at a very different level within the PCGs studied. Members of the case study PCG recognised the relative strengths of each of the professional groups represented on the Board and realised that, if used efficiently, could contribute towards the effective development of the PCG. In the neighbouring PCGs there was evidence of group conflict and lack of team-working.

The enhancement of the skills highlighted above and others which emerged during the study (budgetary control, leadership, managing meetings, negotiation skills, performance management, change management, commissioning, decision making, human resource management, strategic planning, time management) are essential if PCGs are to fulfil their role and develop. Training courses are being made available to PCGs but lack of time may result in some members being reluctant to attend. Also this research highlighted that members have varying training needs and some elements of a formal training course could be irrelevant. Training which members could 'dip into' as required would be seen to be of value and would not draw on the limited time available.

It is planned that PCGs will work together towards developing clinical governance and share best practice as recommended in the White Paper, *The New NHS – Modern, Dependable* (DoH, 1997). We propose that this concept be extended to enable PCGs to share non-clinical innovative best practice.

Not only are effective working relationships required within each PCG but also between the PCGs and the local health authority. One disturbing finding of this study was that all PCGs contacted indicated that the local health authority was hindering the development of PCGs throughout the region. However, since this research has been completed the importance of the role of Health Authorities in supporting PCGs has been emphasised by John Denham, Minister for Health (DoH, 2000).

Finally, it must be acknowledged that this was an exploratory study of a new structure. Further research is required using a larger sample covering other regions so that detailed statistical analysis can be carried out. Also many of the PCGs in the comparative study pointed out that it was early days for their Boards. A longitudinal approach would trace the development of these PCGs and demonstrate to what extent they had adopted best practice.

References

Association of Community Health Councils for England and Wales (1998), 'Primary Care Groups – The Early Guidance', *Health News Briefing*, London.

Denzin, N.K. (1970), *The Research Act in Sociology*, Butterworth, London.

Department of Health (1997), *The New NHS – Modern, Dependable*, HMSO, London.

Department of Health (1998), *Saving Lives, Our Healthier Nation*, HMSO, London.

Department of Health (2000), *Developing Prime Care Groups*, Department of Health, London

Department of Health (2000), *Primary Care Groups*, NHS Executive, 19 April, http://www.doh.gov.uk/pricare/pcgs.htm.

Gilley, J. (1999), 'Meeting the Information and Budgetary Requirements of Primary Care Groups', *British Medical Journal*, Vol. 318, pp. 168–70.

Harding, S. and Long, T. (1998), *MBA Management Models*, Gower Publishing, England.

Malhotra, N.K. and Birks, D.F. (1998), *Marketing Research: An applied approach*, Pearson Education, Harlow.

Miles, M.B. and Huberman, A.M. (1994), *Qualitative Data Analysis*, Sage, California.

Stake, R.E. (1998), 'Case Studies', in N.N. Denzin and Y.S. Lincoln (eds.), *Strategies for Qualitative Enquiry*, Sage, California, pp. 86–109.

Strauss, A. (1987), *Qualitative Analysis for Social Scientists*, Cambridge University Press, New York.

Streubert, H.J. and Carpenter, D.R. (1995), *Qualitative Research in Nursing: Advancing the humanistic imperative*, Lippincott, Philadelphia.

Yin, R.K.(1984), *Case Study Research: Design and methods*, Applied Social Research Methods Series, Vol. 5, Sage, California.

Chapter Eight

The Role of Middle Managers in Realising Human Resource Strategy: Evidence from the NHS

Graeme Currie and Stephen Procter

Introduction

The Interaction of Personnel with Middle Managers in the NHS

The discussion of the interaction of middle or line management with the personnel function was fuelled by the debate about the emergence of human resource management (Poole, 1990; Sisson, 1990; Storey, 1992). Storey (1992, p. 214), for example, says that 'contrary to speculative reports about the demise of the middle manager, occupants of these roles were exercising authority across a greatly expanded territory'.

More recently, the idea that the personnel function carries out its role in collaboration with line managers has gained more prominence from publicity afforded to Ulrich's (1997) book, *Human Resource Champions*. Ulrich sets out multiple roles that the personnel function should take on. These are operational as well as strategic, with the potential for the latter dependent upon effective discharge of the former. This model carries with it implications for the personnel professional's relationship with line management. Most importantly, Ulrich recognises the role line managers can play in the delivery of HR policy. Thus although in this model the personnel function is responsible for the accomplishment of the deliverables, it does not have to do all the actual work. Instead, the work will be shared to a significant extent with line managers.

Ulrich's framework for realising human resource strategy has been highlighted as a prescriptive model for the personnel function in the NHS by

Organisation Development in Health Care: Strategic Issues in Health Care Management, R.K. Rushmer, H.T.O. Davies, M. Tavakoli and M. Malek (eds), Ashgate Publishing Ltd, 2002.

Hugh Taylor, its Director of Human Resources, in numerous speeches across the country to health service personnel practitioners. Despite this, it does not appear to be the case that the importance of middle managers, as part of the cadre of line managers, is recognised by the personnel function in the NHS.

The process of reform following the Griffiths Report (DHSS, 1983) appeared to offer both the personnel function and middle managers a good chance to take on a more strategic role. The role of management was in general being enhanced, trusts were being established and were encouraged to act autonomously, and labour costs, flexibility and pay were high on the agenda. However, a more strategic role for the personnel function went unrealised (Bach, 1994; Caines, 1990; Guest and Peccei, 1992, 1994), as did an enhanced role for middle managers. Important in this were attacks upon middle managers in the NHS since the mid-1990s (Hancock, 1994; *Health Service Journal*, 1994a, 1994b), which reflect more general organisational trends to restructure and 'thin out' layers of management (Drucker, 1988; Kanter, 1989; Peters, 1987, 1992).

What has not been apparent in the NHS is the hope expressed by, amongst others, Frohman and Johnson (1993) and Smith (1997), that, following de-layering, the remaining middle managers can have an enhanced role. To illuminate this within the area of human resource strategy we turn to the strategic change literature and the typology of middle management involvement developed by Floyd and Wooldridge (1992, 1994, 1997).

The Conceptual Framework

Approaches to strategic change in the NHS have traditionally separated the formulation of strategic change from its implementation, with the former remaining the preserve of executive management. As a result there has been little consideration of a role for middle managers beyond that of merely implementing deliberate strategy. In contrast, a processual approach (Mintzberg and Waters, 1985; Pettigrew et al., 1992), in which strategy represents a set of pragmatic compromises between various stakeholders in the organisation (Pettigrew, 1985), allows for a much greater middle management role.

Floyd and Wooldridge's framework (1992, 1994, 1997) is useful in classifying the forms this role can take. They outline a typology of involvement in strategic change which distinguishes between upward and downward influence. In terms of upward influence, the roles taken on by middle managers are 'championing alternatives' (see also Kanter, 1982; Burgelman, 1983a,

1983b) and 'synthesising information' (Nonaka, 1988). The former is seen as a product of ideas divergent from organisation thinking, whereas the latter is more integrative, since middle managers interpret and evaluate information concerning internal and external events. As regards downward influence – that is, the carrying out of strategy (Schilit, 1987; Schendel and Hofer, 1979) – middle managers 'facilitate adaptability' and 'implement deliberate strategy'. The former may be divergent, since here the middle manager is concerned to nourish adaptability apart from the plans embedded in deliberate strategy (Bower, 1970; Kanter, 1983). The latter is often considered the key strategic role of middle managers (Nutt, 1987; Schendel and Hofer, 1979) and is defined as managerial interventions that align organisational action with strategic intentions.

The Case

Our case study organisation, Edwards Hospital, is an acute hospital. Its annual budget at the time of data-gathering was £114 million and it employed around 5,000 staff. Edwards Hospital is structured around 32 clinical directorates and five non-clinical directorates.

We can define middle managers as those who 'mediate, negotiate and interpret connections between the organisation's institutional (strategic) and technical (operational) levels' (Floyd and Wooldridge, 1997, p. 466). A distinction is necessary between those middle managers that work within specialist functions, such as marketing and human resources, and those who work within operations but also perform the coordinating role. This chapter focuses upon the latter, a group which in Edwards Hospital consists of 32 clinical directors, 13 specialty managers and 12 nurse managers. Representatives of this group were interviewed in three directorates of the hospital.

This chapter reports upon findings from one of these, the Theatres Directorate, and of particular interest is a major human resource intervention in this area, the so-called Theatres Project. This involved the harmonisation of terms and conditions of the nurses and the theatre practitioner (ODAs), two groups of employees who essentially carried out similar jobs. The harmonisation was achieved by implementing competence-based job descriptions and a new local pay scheme.

The personnel function in Edwards is called the Human Resources (HR) Department and is headed by a Director of Human Resources. He has a place on the Trust Board alongside five other executive directors and the chief executive. He does not have voting rights at board meetings, although, as he explained, 'it rarely comes to this'. Much of the responsibility for the relationship between the personnel function and middle managers lies with the Personnel Manager, who reports into the Director and deputises for him when necessary. Into the Personnel Manager report three Personnel Advisors, who spend much of their time out in the directorates to which they are attached, working alongside middle managers.

Formal human resource strategy is set out in a document, 'Human Resource Strategy 1998–2003'. Key themes are identified, and this is followed by some more specific objectives. A statement within the strategy document outlines the role of the corporate centre and emphasises that middle management contribution is crucial to its realisation:

> A strategy should describe a method of achieving certain aims and objectives as well as describing those aims and objectives. The implementation of the strategy is the responsibility of numerous managers within the Trust who have responsibilities for human resources. There are certain aims that will only be achieved if corporate action is taken and the role of the Human Resources Department will be to ensure that action is taken when necessary and to give the appropriate support and advice to managers to enable the strategy to be implemented (p. 3).

Findings

The Theatres Project provides an example of the way in which middle managers were involved in strategic change, and it illustrates some of the conditions necessary to allow them to take up an enhanced role. On the one hand, the project showed that middle managers can resist the deliberate strategy of executive management; on the other, we can see that middle managers can be included in strategic change in a way that enhances their role.

Of particular interest in Theatres was that the implementation of local pay had been tackled in two distinct phases, each reflecting a different approach. During the first phase local pay was high on the national agenda for change in the NHS. However, in the second phase the election of a new Labour government introduced a great deal of uncertainty regarding intentions towards pay arrangements. In the first phase, the HR Department, in a drive to ensure consistency across the hospital and wanting directorates to implement a generic framework for local pay, took a top-down approach. Only belatedly did it recognise that this approach to strategic change, which emphasised the more formal and deliberate elements of strategy, was unlikely to be successful:

> In the early days of local pay we drove it from the top but it didn't address their [middle managers] needs and their objectives and therefore they felt that they couldn't support it and take it forward. We did set it up as a very corporate project because it was driven nationally. We did all the classic structural hierarchy things. In retrospect we would have done it differently (Personnel Manager).

As a result, middle managers were able to resist the generic pay and conditions frameworks on the basis that they didn't fit operational context. Middle managers in Theatres stressed that:

> What we needed in Theatres did not run with what Human Resources wanted to run. They kept saying, 'it was for the whole hospital' and we said, 'well, it won't work for us. We'll have to be an exception on this one (Clinical Director: Theatres).

Eventually, in the face of middle manager resistance to its top-down imposition, the HR Department allowed the middle managers to have significant influence over local pay and conditions developed for the theatres area.

At the same time, government policy was increasingly emphasising financial constraint, requesting year-on-year efficiency gains. The HR Department highlighted the impact of this upon strategic change:

> It's all about the bottom line today and not necessarily investing in the future. I believe in the longer-term, over five or six years, we could save thousands of pounds by introducing harmonised pay and conditions into nursing by reducing turnover, vacancies, induction, but it isn't real money this year (Personnel Manager).

As a result of the financial constraints facing the trust, any local pay initiative 'had to make sound business sense' (Director of Human Resources). Middle managers were therefore more likely to be included in the formulation of strategic change, because 'middle managers input was required at an early stage so that a business case could be made' (Director of Human Resources). In addition, government policy towards local pay became uncertain and there was no centrally driven prescription in the area. As a result, and in contrast to earlier days when they were driven by the HR Department, both the direction and detail of local pay were driven by middle managers:

> We decided what we wanted to do. We mapped people's salaries. We had meetings with our staff in which Human Resources were involved. We wrote forms and letters: 'This is the package. This is your offer' (Specialty Manager: Theatres).

So we went to the board with the Theatres Project fully costed – £30,000 best case, £60,000 worst case etc – and worked closely with Theatres management to ensure we met these figures. They [Theatres management] had to be involved right at the start because there was so much nitty gritty work to be done (Director of Human Resources).

Middle manager involvement was encouraged by a statement in the strategy document that set out a key theme of 'encourag[ing] more flexible working practices aimed at the delivery of quality patient care'. Within this, the main objective was to 'create new roles and review boundaries between jobs on the basis of service needs and effective delivery of care to patients'. The middle managers enjoyed an enhanced role in two ways in relation to this strategic theme. First, they were included in its development, through membership of a working group that formulated drafts of the document. This provided boundary-spanning opportunities for middle managers:

I have recently been on a working group – it's a cross-section of the hospital – that's looked at the Human Resources Strategy that will take us forward from 1998 for five years, looking at corporate direction and objectives and how we need to develop the workforce to try to achieve that strategic direction. We looked at various drafts of the document and put our comments forward. We weren't actually writing from scratch (Specialty Manager: Theatres).

Second, they both elaborated upon the broad theme set out in formal strategy so that it fitted operational context and developed the means by which such ends were realised. In Theatres the HR Department provided the initial impetus regarding local pay through broad statements in the formal strategy document, but the project would not have succeeded had there not been specific operational problems that local managers wanted to solve. In order to encourage teamworking, for example, 'we would need to produce a rota that would work for both groups [nurses and theatre practitioners] of staff, as a result of which pay and conditions would need to be harmonised' (Theatres Manager). Therefore Theatres managers 'insisted' that local pay be implemented despite its being put on the back-burner nationally:

A long time ago we wanted to do something about it and we were told, 'Wait for local pay'. And we sat back and we waited. Nothing progressed. Eventually I think HR got tired of waiting as well and asked for pilot sites. So we said, 'Can we be the pilot for local pay? Because we really need to sort this problem of Whitley anomalies' (Specialty Manager: Theatres).

Middle managers in Theatres developed a single pay spine and decided how staff would fit into it:

> We decided there would be several bands, gave them numbers and fitted 170 staff into it. The majority of our trained nurses fit into band 6, which is the old nursing grades of D and E. Our direct entry ODAs [theatre practitioners] come in here [demonstrated on chart as 5], which is a massive jump when they are qualified. Porters, auxiliaries and clerks fit into band 2. We haven't got charge hands, the old A&C [Administrative and Clerical] 3 grades who might go into band 3 and we don't use 4 at all (Nurse Manager: Theatres).

Discussion and Conclusions

In this intervention in Edwards Hospital, the HR Department successfully realised its objectives when it worked through and negotiated with middle managers (Barnett et al., 1996; Ulrich, 1997). As a result, middle managers enjoyed an enhanced role in the realisation of human resource strategy in two of the ways identified by Floyd and Wooldridge (1992, 1994, 1997): through increased discretion in 'implementing deliberate strategy', because they determined the means to meet broad ends; and through 'synthesising information' to contribute towards the initial formulation of those broad ends. Their contribution in these roles came about because of their knowledge of operational context.

Influence such as this, which was integrative with corporate strategy, appeared more appropriate on the basis that it did not alter the overall direction of the organisation but was instead concerned to leverage resources within it. While it might not represent influence upon broad corporate strategy, it represents influence upon the strategic subsystem level of Edwards Hospital. The way in which theatre practitioner and nurse performance was linked to pay, the stretching of resources, and the fact that it matched demands from customers for patient-focused care, all gave the theatre services in Edwards some advantage over neighbouring hospitals.

Taking into account the corporate strategy that local pay be introduced, middle managers worked out the impact of local pay upon budgets to make a business case for its introduction. The role of the HR Department was initially one of providing a broad philosophy and framework within which middle manager discretion would determine the details. Even in this, middle managers from all areas of the hospital were involved as working group members, and it was middle managers who developed the single pay spine. They also worked out implications for individual's pay, managed the problems associated with this, and developed the appeals mechanisms for staff.

It should be noted that while there was emergent strategic change that emanated from middle managers in Edwards Hospital, such influence was more likely where it was consistent with the corporate vision, which in turn was determined by an increasingly prescriptive central government policy. For example, central government policy, initially at least, encouraged trusts to adopt local pay as part of a more businesslike approach to health care provision but, at the same time, required that change be cost-neutral as part of a drive for efficiency gains.

To help ensure consistency with central government policy, the HR Department provided frameworks, such as the formal HR strategy, within which emergent change could took place. As a result, to ensure convergence between emergent strategic change and the dictates of central government there appeared little opportunity for middle managers to take on a divergent role of 'facilitating adaptability' or 'championing alternatives' (Floyd and Wooldridge, 1992, 1994, 1997).

Thus we can see that middle managers can enjoy considerable influence in the realisation of strategic change in the area of human resource strategy. This influence lies in the roles of implementing deliberate strategy and synthesising information. To help overcome external constraints and for middle managers to enjoy an enhanced role, certain characteristics of organisational context may need to be present. What we have seen as helpful in this case is that strategic change combined deliberate and emergent elements and the formulation and implementation of strategic change were intertwined.

So what of the future role of middle managers in strategic change? There is a growing body of work in the general management literature that suggests middle managers can add value to organisations (Frohman and Johnson, 1993; Smith, 1997). While the majority of academic commentators in the health services management field have not noted this, the findings from this case illustrate that middle managers can take on an enhanced role. Furthermore, although we are in the early days of the Labour government reforms, there does appear to be a shift towards more collaborative relationships between purchasers and providers, in which networks rather than markets or hierarchies are emphasised (Hunter, 1998; Kirkpatrick, 1999; Rhodes, 1997). While the growth of the networking phenomenon has paradoxically been the result of central government intervention (Ferlie and Pettigrew, 1998), an enhanced middle manager role in the new arrangements may require that central government intervene less than during previous reforms. Whether the current government is less likely than the previous administrations to intervene is questionable. As Klein (1999, p. 9) notes, 'Labour's new NHS represents a reversion to a command and control model'. Further, the Labour government is committed to budget austerity and to a greater visibility for performance in the NHS. This may work against an enhanced role for middle managers.

References

Bach, S. (1994), 'Restructuring the Personnel Function: The case of NHS trusts', *Human Resource Management Journal*, 5 (2), pp. 99–115.

Barnett, S., Buchanan, D., Patrickson, M. and Maddern, J. (1996), 'Negotiating the Evolution of the HR Function: Practical advice from the health care sector', *Human Resource Management Journal*, 6 (4), pp. 18–37.

Bower, J. (1970), *Managing the Resource Allocation Process*, Harvard University Press, Cambridge, Mass.

Burgelman, R. (1983a), 'A Model of the Interaction of Strategic Behaviour, Corporate Context, and the Concept of Strategy', *Academy of Management Review*, 8 (1), pp. 61–70.

Burgelman, R. (1983b), 'A Process Model of Internal Corporate Venturing in a Diversified Major Firm', *Administrative Science Quarterly*, 28, pp. 223–44.

Caines, E. (1990), 'Time to Grow Up: Message from the top for NHS personnel managers', *Personnel Management*, August, p. 12.

Currie, G. (1999a), 'Resistance Around a Management Development Programme: Negotiated order in a hospital trust', *Management Learning*, 30 (1), pp. 43–62.

Currie, G. (1999b), 'The Influence of Middle Managers in the Business Planning Process', *British Journal of Management*, 10 (2), pp. 141–56.

Currie, G. (2000), 'The Role of Middle Managers in Strategic Change – the case of marketing in the NHS', *Public Money and Management*, 20 (1), pp. 17–21.

Department of Health and Social Security (DHSS) (1983), *NHS Management Inquiry* (Griffiths Report), HMSO, London.

Drucker, P. (1988), 'The Coming of the New Organization', *Harvard Business Review*, 66 (1), pp. 45–53.

Floyd, S. and B. Wooldridge (1992), 'Middle Management Involvement in Strategy and its Association with Strategic Type: A research note', *Strategic Management Journal*, 13, pp. 153–67.

Floyd, S. and Wooldridge, B. (1994), 'Dinosaurs or Dynamos? Recognising Middle Management's Strategic Role', *Academy of Management Executive*, 8 (4), pp. 47–57.

Floyd, S. and Wooldridge, B. (1997), 'Middle Management's Strategic Influence and Organisational Performance', *Journal of Management Studies*, 34 (3), pp. 465–85.

Frohman, A. and Johnson, L. (1993), *The Middle Management Challenge: Moving from crisis to empowerment*, McGraw-Hill, New York.

Guest, D. and Peccei, R. (1992), *The Effectiveness of Personnel Management in the NHS*, NHS Personnel Development Division, London.

Guest, D. and Peccei, R. (1994), 'The Nature and Causes of Effective Human Resource Management', *British Journal of Industrial Relations*, 32 (3), pp. 219–41.

Hancock, C. (1994), 'Managers Out for the Count', *Health Service Journal*, 105, 5384, p. 17.

Health Service Journal (1994a), 'Experts Warn against Lack of Leadership in the NHS', 104, 5427, p. 3.

Health Service Journal (1994b), 'The First Lesson for Margaret Beckett', 104, 5427, p. 15.

Hunter, D. (1998), 'Putting the National in the NHS', *Health Service Journal*, 108, 5590, p 18.

Kanter, R. (1982), 'The Middle Manager as Innovator', *Harvard Business Review*, July–August, pp. 95–105.

Kanter, R. (1983), *The Change Masters: Corporate entrepreneurs at work*, Routledge, London.

Kanter, R. (1989), *When Giants Learn to Dance*, Simon & Schuster, New York.

Kirkpatrick, I. (1999), 'The Worst of Both Worlds? Public Services without markets or bureaucracies', *Public Money and Management*, 19 (4), pp. 7–14.

Klein, R. (1999), 'Grating Expectations', *The Guardian*, 20 October, pp. 8–9.

Mintzberg, H. and Waters, J. (1985), 'Of Strategies Deliberate and Emergent', *Strategic Management Journal*, 6, pp. 257–72.

Nonaka, I. (1988), 'Towards Middle Up/Down Management: Accelerating information creation', *Sloan Management Review*, 29, pp. 9–18.

Nutt, P. (1987), 'Identifying and Appraising how Managers Install Strategy', *Strategic Management Journal*, 8, pp. 1–14.

Peters, T. (1987), *Thriving on Chaos*, Harper & Row, New York.

Peters, T. (1992), *Liberation Management*, Macmillan, New York.

Pettigrew, A. (1985), *The Awakening Giant*, Blackwell, Oxford.

Pettigrew, A., Ferlie, E. and McKee, L. (1992), *Shaping Strategic Change*, Sage, London.

Poole, M. (1990), 'Editorial: HRM in an international perspective', *International Journal of Human Resource Management*, 1 (1), pp. 1–15.

Procter, S. and Currie, G. (1999), 'The Role of the Personnel Function: Roles, perceptions and processes in an NHS trust', *International Journal of Human Resource Management*, 10(6), pp. 1077–91.

Rhodes, R. (1997), 'From Marketization to Diplomacy: It's the mix that matters', paper to Public Service Research Unit Annual Conference, Cardiff Business School, Cardiff.

Schendel, D. and Hofer, C. (1979), *Strategic Management: A new view of business policy and planning*, Little, Brown & Co, Boston, Mass.

Schilit, W. (1987), 'An Examination of the Influence of Middle Level Managers in Formulating and Implementing Strategic Decisions', *Journal of Management Studies*, 24, pp. 271–93.

Sisson, K. (1990), 'Introducing the Human Resource Management Journal', *Human Resource Management Journal*, 1 (1), pp. 1–11.

Smith, V. (1997), *Managing in the Corporate Interest: Control and resistance in an American bank*, University of California Press, Berkeley.

Storey, J. (1992), *Developments in the Management of Human Resources*, Blackwell, Oxford.

Ulrich, D. (1997), *Human Resource Champions*, Harvard Business School Press, Boston, Mass.

Chapter Nine

Effective and Ineffective Leadership within the NHS in Wales

Paula Palmer

Leadership Demands

More than ever, organisations challenge leaders to think at a higher level of intellectual complexity. Organisations need to be global and local at the same time, to be small in some ways but big in others, to be centralised some of the time and decentralised most of it. They expect their workers to be more autonomous and more of a team, their managers to be more delegating and more controlling.

Such a dynamic context requires leaders to capture the benefits of seemingly opposing forces such as ensuring both stability and change, of pursuing a vision whilst managing the reality, and has usefully been described as the 'theory of opposites' (Handy, 1994). It portrays the constant white-water that leaders are expected to navigate, and provides a backdrop for the challenges facing them both in ensuring long term success and adopting an optimal leadership style to achieve it.

Leadership Style

The basic challenge of leadership is to engage the minds and efforts of individuals so they will want to work toward a particular goal, and so they will begin to think differently about that goal and their relationship to the organisation.

Leaders have discovered that to enhance their own ability to lead, they must encourage development of leadership skills in their 'followers'. This requires a shift in the way we think about work and roles: it requires a

Organisation Development in Health Care: Strategic Issues in Health Care Management, R.K. Rushmer, H.T.O. Davies, M. Tavakoli and M. Malek (eds), Ashgate Publishing Ltd, 2002.

transformation in our understanding of leadership and the leadership processes, as well as an awareness of leadership psychology.

Leadership research during the last two decades (Bass, 1981) has noted that a leaders goal should be *to transform the job and the person so that more than just the work gets done*. Leaders want the tasks to be accomplished and they want them to be fulfilling, rewarding, and satisfying to the employers. The term 'transformational leadership' has been adopted to embrace this concern of, and describe the activities required of, millennium leaders.

A Shift towards Transformational Leadership

Transformational leadership, it appears, is now the required and most effective style of our NHS leaders, as compared to an exclusively traditional, top-down, 'bridge to engine-room' approach. This traditional style, termed 'transactional leadership' uses the relative status and power of leaders and followers to establish transactions and exchanges between leader and follower for the undertaking of work.

Transformational leadership illustrates how the relationship between follower and leader is 'transformed' from exchanges, by appealing to the higher needs of the follower(s). These include the emotional needs, the development and empowerment of followers and establishing a sense of individual responsibility, control and destiny.

Transformational leadership has been usefully described (Bass, ibid.) as the 'Four Is':

- *idealised attributes and behaviours ('charisma')* refers to the quality some leaders have of embodying role models that followers want to emulate. They can be counted on to the right thing, demonstrate high levels of ethical and moral conduct, avoiding power for personal gain;
- *inspirational motivation* refers to the ability of leaders to motivate those around them by providing meaning and challenging their followers' work. The leader shares a vision, communicating expectations that followers want to meet;
- *intellectual stimulation* describes how a leader stimulates followers' efforts to be innovative and creative, through questioning assumptions and reframing problems, without criticism;
- *individualised consideration* refers to how leaders pay special attention to each individual's needs for achievement and growth by acting as coach or

mentor. New learning opportunities are created along with a supportive climate, with an acceptance of individual differences.

In contrast, the more traditional transactional leadership style is based on a series of exchanges or bargains between leaders and followers. A common typology of transactional leadership includes:

- *contingent reward*, where followers are rewarded through merit increases or bonuses in recognition of meeting explicit objectives;
- *management by exception (MBE)* – *'active'*, where the leader arranges to actively monitor deviance from standards, mistakes and errors; whilst
- *MBE* – *'passive'* implies waiting for deviances and then taking corrective action;
- *laissez-faire* leadership is considered the avoidance or absence of leadership.

Research Objectives

As leadership is one of the most important factors determining the success and survival of groups and organisations, it is of little wonder that the study of leadership has engaged researchers over the last 60 years or so. However, despite the extensive research into the field, empirical studies have largely ignored the biggest employer in Europe.

This study was undertaken to further the understanding of leadership theory and research within the unique context of the health service, and compare findings with those of private sector research. The primary objective was to identify common observable behaviours of leaders which contribute to perceptions of the most and least effective leadership styles.

Conducted within the National Health Service in Wales, the study further differed from most prior research in that:

1 the *full range* of leadership styles (Avolio and Bass, 1991), including transformational and transactional styles, were measured, including the *effects* of leadership styles on followers;
2 data were collated from *peers, subordinates and superiors of leaders*, across a range of managerial strata and professions; and crucially;
3 perceptions of *both effective and ineffective leader styles* were examined simultaneously, to facilitate a direct and immediate comparison.

Design and Methodology

A postal survey of perceptions of leadership efficacy used two copies of the Multifactor Leadership Questionnaire (Bass and Avolio, 1990) which were counterbalanced across the sample. Participants were required to rate the 'most effective' and 'least effective' leaders they knew well enough to describe, having worked with or observed each. 107 subjects, (66 per cent male, 34 per cent female; age range 25–69 years) responded, representing eight recognised levels of management. All participants had completed an executive development programme appropriate to their profession, and were considered interested and knowledgeable in leadership issues.

Outcome Measures

The study utilised the repeated measures multivariate analysis of variance to ascertain overall interaction between perceptions and leadership styles, whilst Tukey's post hoc test was subsequently used to confirm significant differences between the two leadership styles and effects on followers.

Findings

There has been a considerable amount of work examining effective leadership styles (Bennis, 1884; Hogan et al., 1994) and male-female differences in leadership styles (Eagly, 1981; Alimo-Metcalfe, 1991). Nonetheless, results from the present study represent the first substantial repeated measures empirical investigation of both effective and ineffective leaders style differences within the NHS in Wales.

The results of the study confirmed that the most effective leader style in the NHS is the equivalent of that within the private / commercial sector. In addition, the findings of the study extend the validity of Bass's leadership research and model in three specific ways.

1   *'Most effective' leaders were described as exhibiting significantly more transformational* behaviours than 'least effective' leaders. Further analysis of this overall effect was undertaken by considering the nine measures of leadership behaviour (five transformational; four transactional, as described

above), which revealed a hierarchical model of effective leader behaviours, as represented in Figure 9.1.

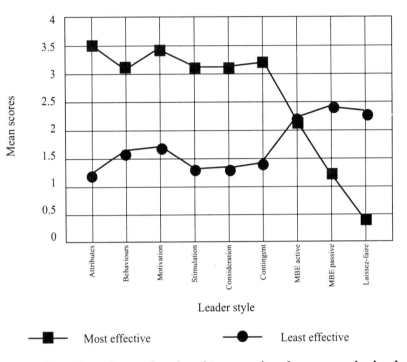

Figure 9.1   Transformational and transactional measures by leader type

'Most effective' leaders were described as almost equally displaying 'idealised behaviour', 'individual consideration' and 'intellectual stimulation'. Highest scores were obtained for 'idealised attributes' and 'inspirational motivation'. The measures of 'idealised attributes' and 'individual consideration' provided the strongest differentiators *between* leader types.

2 *A three-dimensional model of 'optimal leadership style' emerged* which supported Avolio and Bass's (ibid.) model. The results suggest that the optimal leadership style utilises the full range of leadership style, including transformational and transactional behaviours.

Indeed, according to Avolio and Bass's model, the more active role a leader takes, the more effective their style. The most active style of leadership, according to the model, is a transformational one.

3 *Leader type was significantly correlated to follower effectiveness.* 'Most
   Effective' leaders scored significantly higher on the three measures of
   'Augmentation' - follower effectiveness within the job, followers exerting
   extra effort, and their satisfaction with leader style.

Results from the study thus further validated the 'falling dominoes effect'
(Bass et al., 1987) of effective leadership where individual effort and
performance beyond normal expectations is noted, even when the
(transformational) leader is absent.

Thus the study confirmed the need for a dynamic interplay between the
transformational and transactional leadership styles. It revealed that effective
leaders were regarded as exhibiting a preponderance of transformational
leadership styles, which were supported by, but to a much lesser extent,
transactional styles.

Two unexpected results were revealed in Figure 9.1. Firstly that most
effective leaders scored significantly more highly on 'contingent reward' than
least effective leaders, despite the measure being typically categorised within
a transactional framework. In addition, both most and least effective leaders
scored very similar scores on 'active management-by-exception', again
typically regarded as within the domain of transactional behaviour. These
results, in particular, illustrate an optimum balance of these factors in
leadership:

* *contingent reward.* Establishing clear expectations from followers, but
  balanced by the freedom and empowerment established through transformational leadership, thus allowing the follower to work within the parameters
  as they see best. This is in contrast to the traditional understanding of
  contingent reward as one which has represented an exchange of financial
  rewards for the successful delivery of agreed objectives;
* *active management-by-exception.* The monitoring of followers performance
  and efforts, balanced by providing encouragement and support for improved
  performance, through reflection and learning from the experience. This is
  in contrast to the traditional approach of persistent monitoring and
  correction of performance etc. without the opportunity for reflection.

Finally, two findings contradict current leadership research within the
private sector. Firstly, within the current, public sector study, the most effective
and 'transformational' leaders were more likely to be perceived as those at
the top of the organisation, rather than throughout the organisation.

Secondly, the results revealed that perceptions of effective leadership within the NHS remains gender-segregated. Research that asserts that females are more likely than men to exhibit a transformational leadership style (Rosener, 1990) is not fully supported. Whilst examples of 'most effective' leadership did include female examples (17 per cent of total leader sample) Schein's work, (e.g. 1973) reporting the stereotyping of men as more effective leaders, was supported by the current study ; significantly more male participants used a male example as an effective leader than a female example, despite Rosener's (ibid.) findings.

Conclusions

It is encouraging that transformational leadership is perceived as the most effective style within the health service. However, there are several implications for the NHS:

- *leader selection*: as we have noted, transformational leadership is regarded as the most effective leadership style. It is therefore imperative that the identification and selection of the current and future leaders is driven by appropriate selection criteria and competencies. In a recent research, Alimo-Metcalfe (1999) reminds us that transactional leadership has proven easier to observe and measure in the past, and cautions that any attempt to reduce transformational leadership into competencies promises to be fraught with difficulty, due to its complex nature.

    Certainly, criteria should avoid the task- and skill-based framework, and the development of a holistic, values and qualities-driven framework will prove a worthwhile challenge. Indeed the hierarchical model of effective behaviours revealed in the current study could provide a useful starting point;
- *leader development*: the promotion of leaders within the NHS and throughout the organisation is fundamental to the success of the health service. Human resource policies and practices need to be reviewed to reflect current research; management and leadership development programmes should encourage and inform participants of intrinsic qualities of transformational leadership. Certainly, self-awareness of one's own style would provide a bedrock for leadership development. The three-dimensional leadership model should ensure that chiefly transformational leadership is practised and that less active styles are engaged only as appropriate;

- *female leaders*: purported to be more transformational in style than men, women would seem equally suited to leadership positions. The abrasive, directive manager whose style pushes him/her to the top of an organisation now contradicts recent studies. Once the selection and development implications above are addressed, it is expected that many more women will be established at all leader levels of the organisation.

In summary, the study does not suggest that a wholesale shift in leadership style is required. There is a need for balance: a balance between wholehearted and whole-headed; a union between rational and emotional modes of thinking, and an 'essential tension' between hard minds and soft hearts.

There is widespread and persistent calls for leaders to combine and make the best use of both modes of the apparently opposing styles. A synthesis of these styles is required to meet the contrasting demands placed upon organisations and their leaders. Today's corporate balance requires a different style from either leadership extreme.

References

Alimo-Metcalfe, B. (1991), 'Leadership, Gender and Assessment', paper presented at the European Foundation for Managerial Development Conference on *Rethinking Management, Implications for Organisations in the 1990s*, 9–12 October, Isida, Palmero.

Alimo-Metcalfe, B. (1999), *Effective Leadership*, LGMB, Ref MSO219.

Avolio, B.J. and Bass, B.A. (1991), *The Full-range of Leadership Development*, Center for Leadership Studies, Binghampton University, New York.

Bass, B.M. (1981), *Stodgill's Handbook of Leadership: A survey of theory and research*, Macmillan, New York.

Bass, B.A. and Avolio, B.J. (1990), *Multifactor Leadership Questionnaire*, Consulting Psychologist Press, Palto Alto.

Bass, B.M., Waldman, D.A., Avolio, B.J. and Bebb, M. (1987), 'Transformational Leadership and the Falling Dominoes Effect', *Group and Organisation Studies*, 12, pp. 73–87.

Bennis, W.G. (1984), *Leaders*, Harper Perennial, New York.

Eagly, A.H. (1991), *Sex Differences in Social Behaviour: A social role interpretation*, Lawrence Erlbaum Associates Inc., Hillsdale, New Jersey.

Handy, C. (1994), *The Age of Paradox*, Harvard Business School Press, Boston.

Hogan, R. , Curphy, G.J. and Hogan, J. (1994), 'What we Know about Leadership', *American Psychologist*, June, pp. 493–504.

Rosener, J. (1990), 'Ways Women Lead', *Harvard Business Review*, November–December, pp. 119–25.

Schein, V.E. (1973), 'The Relationship between Role Stereotypes and Requisite Management Characteristics', *Journal of Applied Psychology*, 60, pp. 340–44.

Chapter Ten

Strategic Leadership in Health Care in Challenging Times

M.O. Jumaa and J. Alleyne

Introduction

For the son of a peasant who has grown up within the narrow confines of his village and spends his whole life in the place of his birth, the mode of thinking and speaking characteristics of that village is something that he takes entirely for granted. But for the country lad who goes to the city and adapts himself gradually to city life, the rural mode of living and thinking ceases to be something to be taken-for-granted. He has won a certain detachment from it, and he distinguishes, perhaps quite consciously, between 'rural' and 'urban' modes of thought and ideas ... That which within a given group is accepted as absolute appears to the outsider conditioned by the group situation and recognised as partial. This type of knowledge presupposes a more detached perspective (Mannheim, 1936, p. 81).

This quotation is used by Mannheim to illustrate how our perception of the world and ways of thinking are mediated by social milieu. It also pointed out that the acquisition of new ways of thinking, the adoption of a paradigmatic shift, depends upon a departure from the old-world view. This is the philosophical background and impetus behind the creation of the LEADLAP model. The term – LEADLAP – is used when this model of strategic leadership process is applied, generically, in health care; and the term CLINLAP – clinical nursing leadership learning and action process – is used when the focus of the model is on nursing leadership. This chapter will demonstrate, how LEADLAP – leadership learning and action process – was used within health care education, to facilitate a collaborative understanding of the NHS's cultural web, and how this awareness and action enhanced strategic change implementation.

Hence, it sets out to present and discuss: the LEADLAP model. What is it? Why now and why LEADLAP? What are the advantages of LEADLAP?

Organisation Development in Health Care: Strategic Issues in Health Care Management, R.K. Rushmer, H.T.O. Davies, M. Tavakoli and M. Malek (eds), Ashgate Publishing Ltd, 2002.

What environment is required for LEADLAP to occur so as to be effective? What future research problems surface as a result of implementing LEADLAP?

LEADLAP and Five Strategic Questions

LEADLAP is to be used in conditions of complexity, uncertainty, instability, and an environment where value-conflicts abound. Five strategic questions (5SQs) served as 'path finders' for the user/s to assist and ensure arrival at agreed goals. These questions were:

---

where do we want to go in our health care practice?;

where are we now?;

how can we get to our practice goal?;

which route must we take to get to our goal?; and

what must we do on our journey, and check our progress to ensure that we get to our practice goal?

Box 10.1   Five strategic questions (5SQs)

Each question is explored and answered through a series of relevant sub-questions. The strength of LEADLAP, is that the given situation is managed and led by the application, to the situation, of *true* (they exist), *tried* (they were applied), and *tested* (they worked) strategic management and leadership concepts, tools, theories, frameworks, etc. etc. The goal is to assist to find practical and agreed SMART (specific; measurable; achievable; realistic and relevant; time-bound) solutions, for the project. The strategic management and leadership concepts, theories, and frameworks are always chosen, based on their: *comprehensiveness, consistency*, and *congruity*, when applied to the health care environment. Their evidence credibility was also measured against the extent of their *validity, authenticity, currency, transparency and sufficiency*, when applied to health care practice.

LEADLAP's relationship to the EFQM excellence model is that through *true, tried*, and *tested* strategic management and leadership concepts, it could be used to implement the EFQM model. LEADLAP allows you, through a process of *repetition, representation* and *assistance* (Westley and Mintzberg, 1989) to explore and answer these nine questions, based on the EFQM model:

* to what extent am I an effective leader in health care;

- where is my NHS Trust/PCTs/unit/department heading;
- how well managed are all the staff that I am leading;
- are we adequately resourced for those activities we need to carry out, and are we making the best use of these resources;
- how are we doing things in my NHS Trust/PCTs/unit/department;
- on reflection, and from the feedback we received, are our patients/clients/ users and other customers getting what they need and want from us;
- how satisfied are those who work here, myself included, and what evidence do we have that suggests that the staff and myself want the NHS Trust/ PCTs/unit/department to succeed;
- what is the effect of the activities of my NHS Trust/PCTs/unit/department on the outside world, and do we really care;
- are the staff and myself providing value for money in our services, or are we 'underachieving'? If so what could we do differently?

LEADLAP subscribes to the 'pragmatic school of thought of organisational learning'. Unlike Kolb's learning theory, which tends to focus primarily on individual learning (Kolb et al., 1984), LEADLAP focuses on group as well as individual learning, which is a more natural forum, not only for strategic learning but also for clinical learning. Argyris argues that professionals are highly competent at doing the more routine and technical tasks. However, they are often less competent at dealing with more open-ended, uncertain and ambiguous issues (Argyris, 1993). This is when the double-loop learning opportunity, as configured within LEADLAP would offer health care practitioners a pragmatic strategic tool for health care leadership and strategic organisational learning.

How LEADLAP was Developed

LEADLAP is a product of an Action Science Research Project over a period of 15 months, at the largest Community Healthcare National Health Service (NHS) Trust in England. This very progressive and forward-looking healthcare organisation initially commissioned the Middlesex University in 1995 to provide management and leadership development activities for 46 District Nurse Team Leaders (DNTLs) (District Nurses may be described as public health nurse and similar names are used in other countries). It was later agreed that the 'commission' could be used as a research project. The main purpose of the project was to discover what attitudes, skills, and knowledge are required for the DNTLs to perform their roles effectively, and to begin the development of these characteristics in these clinical team leaders.

A multi-method responsive methodology, including triangulation, was used. This included pre-project diagnostic questionnaires, post-project evaluation questionnaires, data, investigator, theory, and methodological triangulation, as well as open-ended interviews of the clinical team leaders' line managers. The core of the investigation was a series of 2+1+1+1 days workshops and focus groups, spread over 15 months. This approach was appropriate, given that the Primary Health Care environment corresponds to Schon's (1991) concept of 'situations' – i.e. the situation is complex, full of uncertainty, instability, ridden with value-conflicts, yet one of uniqueness.

Why Strategic Leadership Now?

LEADLAP is an idea ripe for its time. Furthermore, in the UK NHS, very radical changes were introduced which led to fundamental shifts in the delivery of health care. How will health and social care in the United Kingdom be delivered as we move beyond the beginning of the twenty-first century? How and where will patients receive their care; and what technological, organisational and demographic changes will influence and mould early twenty-first century health and social care practice? Clearly the future is uncertain, but it is already possible to see that the implications for effective health care management and leadership are potentially wide-ranging, uncertain and very complex. What is however clear, is that the government wants the many health care stakeholders: patients/clients/users; nurses; doctors; managers; pharmacists; radiographers; occupational therapists; etc. etc. within the UK NHS to work together in the delivery of efficient and effective health care (DoH, 1999; DoH, 2000).

The present Labour government has made many public announcements, through several White Papers since coming into office in May 1997. Many of these are positive recognition of the role of the professions and health care managers to 'really' manage the organisation and the delivery of care more efficiently and effectively, now and in this new millennium. The service delivery, organisational and management role for the new NHS required of professionals and managers, are both explicit and implicit in the clinical governance quality performance framework (DoH, 1998c, Figure 2). These are the key drivers that stimulated the need for the use of a strategic leadership approach in health care, to manage and lead in this period of uncertainty.

Why the LEADLAP Approach?

> In an economy where the only certainty is uncertainty, the one sure source of
> lasting competitive advantage is knowledge. When markets shift, technologies
> proliferate, competitors multiply, and products become obsolete almost
> overnight, successful companies are those that consistently create new
> knowledge, disseminate it widely throughout the organisation, and quickly
> embody it in new technologies and products. These activities define the
> 'knowledge-creating' company, whose sole business is continuous innovation.
> (Nonaka, 1991, p. 96).

The context that Nonaka has described also represents the turbulent
environment of the UK's National Health Service (NHS). But the NHS, like
all other organisations, is part of today's context, described by Vaills (1990),
as 'permanent white waters' (unremitting turbulence). Effective leadership,
therefore, must be through a framework that acknowledges, this state of rest-
lessness, as well as the cultural assumptions of the NHS's multiple constituents.
     Strategic health care leadership is defined here as,

> an open process of creative decision-making, which seeks to persuade and
> influence the client, the service user, the customer, and work colleagues to agree
> to the chosen direction in relation to social and health services provision. This
> process is premised on a reflection on the internal, the external and the
> psychological factors impacting on the social and health services (Jumaa and
> Alleyne, 1998b, p. 10).

In the present global knowledge economy, therefore, learning assumes an
important strategic dimension. 'Strategic' in LEADLAP is adopted from
Grundy's (1994) definition of strategy. It is in this context that strategic learning
is used in LEADLAP. It is about resolving messy issues, issues that are usually
complex, uncertain, full of dilemmas, the likes of which are an every day
occurrence in the care arena.

Advantages of the LEADLAP model

Effective implementation of LEADLAP will bring health and social care
organisations, teams and individuals working in the care environment, many
advantages that were never realised under inflexible, rigid and obsolete
approaches. The most significant include:

- developing and sustaining continuous high quality healthcare performance;
- capability development and enhancement of the practitioner, clinician, manager, leader, and carer to link theory with practice; and
- assisting health care managers, leaders, and carers to facilitate the care and clinical leadership processes.

The Environment for LEADLAP

If full benefits are to be gained from using LEADLAP, three **core** conditions are essential:

- health care and clinical staff need to believe in strategic workplace learning for continuous quality performance;
- the achievement of satisfaction for *many* stakeholders involved in the process of health care (recipients and providers, and not just the *key* ones), must become a 'mantra' for all health and social care workers;
- health and social care managers, clinicians and other staff, who agree that, continuous multi-constituents satisfaction is possible only through collaboration amongst *all* of the health and social care practitioners, as well as the patient/clients/users/customers.

Initially, an effective facilitator may be required to facilitate LEADLAP, but the goal of facilitation would be to lead the health care group to self and peer determination, autonomous development and action inquiry in their groups, through self- and peer group supervision. It is clear from this chapter that human resource development and management is, therefore, a key strategic issue, in the race for efficient and effective health and social care, through strategic health and social care leadership (DoH, 1998b).

The research (Jumaa, 1997) that generated LEADLAP discovered that all of the key and significant problems within health and social care teams revolve around:

- problems with goals;
- problems with roles;
- problems with processes;
- problems with relationships.

This is a confirmation of the work of (Moxon, 1993) of how to manage teams,

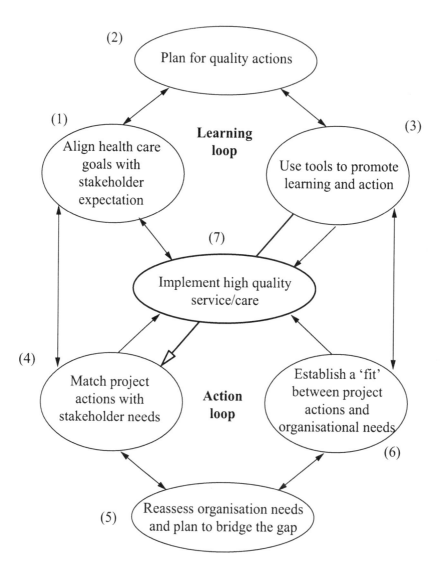

The LEADLAP model has empirically shown that, implemented effectively, strategic care leadership and learning is possible when: health care goals are specific; roles are explicit; processes are clear; and relationships are open.

Figure 10.1 The LEADLAP model

© Jumaa (1999) *Leadership Learning and Action Process*, LEADLAP and Irwin et al.'s (1974 in Moxon 1993) 'hierarchy of team issues'. Both contributed, significantly, to this research process. The research also concluded, with the participants agreement and feedback, that these problems could generally be resolved through ensuring that health and social care and clinical environments have

- specific and agreed goals;
- explicit roles;
- clear processes; and
- open relationships.

It seems clear from the above that an effective and successful implementation requires a dramatic shift from heath and social care practice, as we knew it, in the 'old' NHS. A successful implementation of LEADLAP requires that racism, sexism, ageism, and discrimination based on disabilities, sexuality, accent, class and country of origin, religion, cronyism, nepotism, etc. are not used as the basis to offer rewards and services in the new NHS.

LEADLAP in Action

What follows are references to and from past application of the LEADLAP approach. Particularly, its contribution to the successful validation of the first MSc in Clinical Leadership, in the UK. To facilitate continuous workplace learning, the Project Leader (PL), was given a workbook (similar to those given in the original research of 1996), designed to promote strategic learning, in the workplace. The workbook provided a 'menu' of opportunities for discussions and activities based on the integration of strategic management and leadership theories to workplace experiences. The focus was on supporting the project leader to manage the many demands, constraints, as well as seizing the opportunities that arise, in the course of the project. Five strategic questions (5SQs) served as 'path finders' for the PL to assist and ensure arrival at agreed goals. The key question, therefore, was, to what extent has this approach's contribution to developing actionable knowledge for evidence based health and social care leadership, valid, authentic, current, transparent, and sufficient? (i.e. 'a meta-evidence approach')

Argyris (1993) suggests, that the ultimate test of validity, when creating actionable knowledge, is the extent to which research outcomes can support change intervention in an on-line capacity. 'The truth we assert are a function of our procedural norms which in turn are a function of our shared value system' (Heron, 1981). The Project's activities and results testified to, and led us to conclude, that the approach put forward in this study was valid and has led to actionable knowledge (see Appendix).

Effective facilitation skills in the areas, generally, of intrapersonal, interpersonal, group and emotional management skills were essential for successful implementation of LEADLAP. In this particular project, and because of the nature of the research project, a dramaturgical model of vision, within LEADLAP, was evident. Westley and Mintzberg (1989), using Brook's (1968) work captured all the 'drama' involved in this research process to secure University accreditation for an MSc programme (see Appendix).

Westley and Mintzberg raised a number of intriguing questions: what kind of psychological, social, or technical 'repetition' forms the different visionary styles; what is the exact nature of the symbols and processes visionary leaders employ in their 'representations; what kind of interactions characterise the 'assistance' that the visionary receives from his or her organisation? The process of seeking validation and accreditation for the MSc programme provides us with some of the answers to these intriguing questions. The everyday operationalistion of this evidence based approach to strategic management and leadership is graphically displayed in Figure 10.2.

The greatest danger facing LEADLAP is that health and social care staff may believe that workplace learning needs are the same as any training and development needs. This is not so. LEADLAP's fundamental goal is to position strategic workplace learning as an essential everyday professional and personal development need of achieving continuous, high quality sustainable healthcare performance. LEADLAP seeks to be strategic, pragmatic and realistic in its efforts to establish strategic workplace learning as a core health and social care, clinical, management and leadership process.

Conclusion

This chapter has presented a view of how strategic workplace learning could be positioned to promote and encourage self- and peer determination of professional and personal development, within health and social care organisations, within clinical teams and amongst individuals in the care and clinical environment. Such a situation is feasible through LEADLAP, a strategic care leadership process, based on evidence, developed over a period of fifteen months action research activities with clinical team leaders. It is

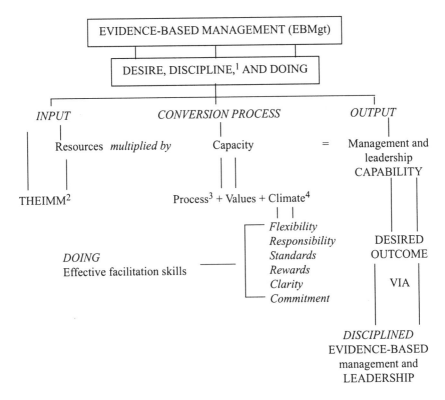

$$\boxed{\text{EVIDENCE-BASED MANAGEMENT (EBMgt)}}$$

$$\boxed{\text{DESIRE, DISCIPLINE,}^1 \text{ AND DOING}}$$

INPUT   *CONVERSION PROCESS*   *OUTPUT*

Resources *multiplied by*   Capacity   =   Management and
                                                    leadership
                                                    CAPABILITY

THEIMM[2]   Process[3] + Values + Climate[4]

                                    ┌── *Flexibility*
DOING   │   *Responsibility*   DESIRED
Effective facilitation skills ──── │   *Standards*   OUTCOME
                                    │   *Rewards*
                                    │   *Clarity*   VIA
                                    └── *Commitment*

                                              DISCIPLINED
                                              EVIDENCE-BASED
                                              management and
                                              LEADERSHIP

1   The Editors, 1999, p. 10.
2   THEIMM stands for resources – time; human; equipment; information; material; money.
     (Jumaa and Alleyne, 1998a).
3   Christensen and Overdorf, 2000, p. 68.
4   Goleman, 2000, p. 81.

Figure 10.2 Evidence-based management and leadership at a glance

proposed as a pragmatic and strategic conceptual tool to manage and lead the present care context. A situation that is fast changing, complex, and extremely difficult to predict.

Could this approach via LEADLAP be classified as a high quality qualitative research? The response is affirmative. It is worth noting however, that unlike the positivist approach where there is an explicit hierarchy of evidence that enables a reviewer to weigh different sources of quantitative data, this is not the case here. This research was about complexity, uncertainty, instability, ambiguity, all processes of organisational change which are more difficult to control than the clinical decisions of the 'scientific' medical practitioners. This research is not about a 'black box' approach. While there is no consensus within the community of organisational behaviour researchers in care, Ferlie et al. (2000) put forward five possible quality indicators:

- good quality work should get beyond pure empiricism so that there should be a relationship with a body of generic *organisational theory*
- there should be an explicit treatment of *methodology and research design.* What methods have been selected and why?
- the *empirical data should have strong internal validity* – that is, 'it should tell it as it really is'
- the high quality work should aim to move beyond purely local studies to *uncover underlying patterns and tendencies across sites*
- high quality work should demonstrate *relevance to practice as well as to theory.*

We believe this research is a quality qualitative research because all the five quality indicators are met. Goleman's (2000) research is our 'evidence' for the quality indicator number four, while the whole stance of the LEADLAP approach itself is about using 'evidence' from *generic organisational theory,* for effective management and leadership (quality indicator number one). LEADLAP is not a prescriptive tool, although it provides a flexible structure. It is about double-loop learning. While it is not linear in its application, its effective use must be iterative in manner. LEADLAP, used effectively, seeks to build a critical mass of health care workplace learning, to discourage the foundation and building of learning islands, and to use workplace learning to promote self- and peer determination in the health and social care work environment.

Choices about care strategy do and can make a difference to the viability, success, and prosperity of health and social care organisations. However, beyond the crucial stages of selecting a viable care strategy and implementing it effectively, is a further sophisticated stage for any care organisation, which could be aptly described as 'learning how to learn'. LEADLAP, the practice of strategic health and social care leadership process, is therefore, concerned primarily with learning how to continuously identify and deal with strategic care issues as they arise. LEADLAP believes that what is genuinely of strategic importance will always change over time, especially with changes in the political government in power.

Care organisations must be cognisant of the fact that strategic workplace learning as a distinctive capability within health care, could be achieved only when there is an explicit realisation that strategic care recipes will not work in dealing with novel strategic health care issues; and that learning to manage the uncertainty and complexity of care involves learning to manage and take risks. Surviving and viability across time involves learning to learn more quickly and putting that learning into action for effective care delivery. It is about effectiveness within familiar problems and contexts, as well as effectiveness within unfamiliar problems and contexts. We can no longer afford to exist within the narrow confines of our creation. We need to learn to let go of obsolete mind-sets. We need to see all health and social care activities afresh.

Acknowledgements

Thanks to: Vari Drennan, Former Head of Nursing Development, Camden and Islington Community Care NHS Trust, who agreed for the 'assignment' to be used, additionally, as a research project; the 46 District Nurse Team Leaders, who took part in the research project; the Clinical Service Managers interviewed; and Mrs Jo Alleyne, for her role as Associate Facilitator.

References

Alleyne, J. and Jumaa, M.O. (1998), 'Work-Based Learning Methodology to Resolve Role Conflict at Work: introducing "Mansour's Matrix"', paper presented at the 6th International Conference on Experiential Learning, *Experiential Learning in the Context of Lifelong Education*, University of Tampere, Finland, 2–5 July.

Argyris, C. (1993), *Knowledge for Action*, Jossey-Bass Publishers, San Francisco.

Brook, P. (1968), *The Empty Space*, Penguin Books, Markham, Ontario.

Christensen, C.M. and Overdorf, M. (2000), 'Meeting the Challenge of Disruptive Change', *Harvard Business Review*, March–April, p. 68.

Department of Health (1998a), *Our Healthier Nation – a Government Green Paper*, HMSO, London.

Department of Health (1998b), *Partnership in Action; New Opportunities for Joint Working between Health and Social Services*, HMSO, London.

Department of Health (1998c), *A First Class Service: Quality in the New NHS*, HMSO, London.

Department of Health (1999), *The Health Act 1999*, HMSO, London.

Department of Health (2000), *The NHS Plan: A plan for investment; A plan for reform*, HMSO, London.

European Foundation for Quality Management (EFQM)(1992), *The European Model for Self-Appraisal,* EFQM, Brussels.

Ferlie, E. et al. (2000), 'Evidence Based Medicine and Organisational Change: An Overview of Some Recent Qualitative Research', paper delivered at the 2nd International OB Research in Health Care, at the Keele University, 26–28 January.

Goleman, D. (2000), 'Leadership that gets Results', *Harvard Business Review*, March–April, p. 81.

Grundy, T. (1994), *Strategic Learning in Action: How to accelerate and sustain business change'*, McGraw-Hill Book Company, London.

Heron, J. (1981), 'Philosophical Basis for a New paradigm', in P. Reason and J. Rowan (eds), *Human Inquiry: A Sourcebook of New Paradigm Research*, John Wiley and Sons, Chichester, pp. 19–35.

Jumaa, M.O (1997), 'Strategic Clinical Team Learning through Leadership', unpublished Research Project Report, part of an MA-WBLS (Strategic Nursing Leadership and Management), Middlesex University.

Jumaa, M.O (1999), 'Nursing Beyond the Year 2000: Towards strategic leadership and learning in nursing', guest paper presented at a CAPITA initiative conference on *The Changing Role of Nurses and GPs: Clinical governance and new partnerships in the new NHS*, April, London.

Jumaa, M.O. and Alleyne, J. (1998b), 'Developing Evidence Based Clinical Nursing Leadership in Primary Health Care', paper presented at the 16th Annual International Conference of the Association of Management, 5–8 August, Fairmont Hotel, Chicago.

Jumaa, M.O.and Alleyne, J.(2000), 'Learning, Unlearning and Relearning: Facilitation in community nursing for delivering the new primary care agenda', paper delivered at the 2nd International OB research in Health Care, 26–28 January, Keele University.

Kolb, D.A. et al. (1984), *Organisational Psychology: An experiential approach*, Prentice-Hall, London.

Mannheim, K. (1936), *Idealogy and Utopia*, cited in Henry, J. (ed.) (1995), *Creative Management*, Sage Publications with The Open University, London.

Moxon, P. (1993), *Building a Better Team*, Gower, Aldershot.

Nonaka, I. (1991), 'The Knowledge-creating Company', *Harvard Business Review*, November–December, pp. 96–104.

Schon, D. (1991) The Reflective Practitioner: How Professionals Think in Action, London. Avery Press.

The Editors (1999) Discipline and Desire, *Harvard Business Review*, July–August, p. 10.

Vaill, P. (1990), *Managing as a Performing Art*, Jossey Bass, San Francisco.

Westley, F. and Mintzberg, H. (1989), Visionary Leadership and Strategic Management., *Strategic Management Journal*, 10, pp. 17–32.

Appendix 1

Specific Strategic Leadership Actions contributing to the Successful Validation of an MSc Clinical Leadership Programme

Specific goals via
Brook's (1968)
'repetition'

- Stating the purpose of the programme development team, based on an
- Understanding of stakeholder issues, analysis and management, leading to
- Deciding and agreeing on SMART goals and objectives (immediate; short and long term)

Explicit roles via
Brook's (1968)
'representation'

- An awareness of the impact of forces in the external environment
- The effect on and of internal politics (within the school and the university), due to changes within the healthcare industry, and the NHS
- Identification of the required resources and capabilities, for the team's viability, and success
- Recognizing internal competition for securing validation for 'prestigious' programme

Clear processes via
Brook's (1968)
'representation'

- SWOT analysis to determine the programme development's team's relative strengths and opportunities
- Knowing the team's key success factors
- Knowing the school's and the university's key success factors
- Identifying the difference between needs and wants and the cost implications
- A working knowledge of the new NHS clinical governance quality framework, and a detailed understanding of the university's quality assurance procedures and processes for new programme development
- Ability to analyse cause and effect of 'open' and 'hidden' staff activities (both academic and support staff)
- Understanding and articulating power issues, and effects on what gets done, by whom, where, when, why, to whom, and how?

Open relationship via
Brook's (1968)
'assistance'

- Management of resistance
- Having the capacity to manage constant change
- 'Mature' and controlled reaction to constant 'changes' to the 'procedures' (changing goal posts' location)
- Demonstrating the ability to work with/change the dominant cultural paradigm
- Challenging and 'dismantling' the 'unprogressive' dominant cultural paradigm
- Making explicit the 'pay-offs' for all participants

Chapter Eleven

Emperor's Clothes? Does Training Pay Off? Evaluating Health Management Training in the Developing World

Zillyham Rojas, Dave Haran and Neil Marr

Introduction

The training programme for middle-management health managers in developing countries evaluated in this study was designed and organised as a three-year project in collaboration between the Liverpool School of Tropical Medicine and the Costa Rican Health and Nutrition Research and Training Institute (INCIENSA). The sponsor of the SIGLOS project was ODA, the Overseas Development Agency of the United Kingdom (now DFID). It included the setting up of the training programme, scholarships for participants from Central America, and financial support to evaluate the effects of the course in participants' workplaces.

It is a success story in some ways but it is still in need of improvement to bring about the desired positive effect.

The training programme is known as SIGLOS, a six-week intensive course offered annually in Costa Rica, employing formal training methods but also Action Learning as its main feature. The project intended that SIGLOS become self-sustaining and run almost entirely by staff from Central America within three years. Academics, researchers and health professionals with appropriate qualifications and experience were identified within the United Kingdom and Central America and invited to contribute to teaching on the course.

SIGLOS was established because management of health services is poor in all Central American countries. The skill level of front line health managers

Organisation Development in Health Care: Strategic Issues in Health Care Management, R.K. Rushmer, H.T.O. Davies, M. Tavakoli and M. Malek (eds), Ashgate Publishing Ltd, 2002.

relies on scarce local training capacity and resources. Very few managers can obtain scholarships for training in developed countries and language barriers are also a major constraint. Reforms to the organisation of health care delivery in Central America make effective training programmes even more urgent.

Formerly, evaluation of health management courses was commonly limited to participants' self-completed, end-of-course questionnaires. No matter how well these assessments are carried out they are of little use in evaluating the impact of training on workplace performance. They also provide little assistance in understanding which aspects of training – policies, design, resources, curricula, training materials, etc. – are relevant to the emerging needs of improving health management in developing countries.

There are many obstacles hampering the evaluation efforts. These include the lack of reliable methods, the high cost of such evaluations and the difficulty in defining and measuring a manager's performance. Perhaps more fundamental is the issue of deciding whether changes in performance are entirely due to the training intervention itself or to extraneous factors such as individual motivation and prevailing incentive structures.

Searching for Methods to Evaluate Health Management Training

A recent World Bank publication stated that current measures are 'of little help in the workplace' (Taschereau, 1998, p. 1).

Evaluation exercises invariably occur far from the real infield day-to-day working world of trainees. Most evaluation material focuses on 'improving' training practice rather than 'proving' its value on the job. Tziner and Haccoun (1991, p. 167) pointed out that 'the ultimate purpose of training evaluation must be to assess the level of on-the-job training transfer'. The Kirkpatrick approach remains the most well known, recommended and used (Phillips, 1983; Graig, 1979).

Questions included, for instance:

- were the participants pleased with the programme? How much information was conveyed to participants (*reaction*);
- what did the participants learn in the programme? What had the participants absorbed and understood (*learning*);
- did the participants change their behaviour based on what was learned (*behaviour*);

- did the change in behaviour positively affect the organisation? Did they produce, for instance, cost savings, work output improvements and/or quality changes (results);
- how do answers to these questions suggest an improved performance out of school in the nitty-gritty workplace?

As Phillips (1983) established, management training is not conducted for the sake of learning something. Its main concern is to bring about positive change in the participants and any impact on his organisation is the only important outcome.

Are there practical ways to measure the impact of training on the performance of the economy? Evaluators confess that suitable methodologies for assessing the broader impact of training are simply not available (Paul, 1983).

Trained health managers' performance can be affected by many variables after a training programme is completed. Common among these confusing factors are the self-motivation of the participant, the environment in which the participant is working and supportive reinforcement from the participant's superiors and organisation. While these vital extras are not directly under the control of most training institutions, this should not be the basis for discarding evaluation. Measurements may not be precise but they are certainly better than no measurement of change at all (Phillips, 1983).

Problem: there is often great difficulty in encouraging management executives to explain how failure occurred or success was attained. Peters (1987) addressed this issue by asking how a 'payment by performance' system could be implemented when performance is so notoriously difficult to measure and, thus, fairly reward.

The Development of the Course on Sistemas de Informacion para la Gerencia local de la Salud (SIGLOS)

The core of the SIGLOS programme was a six-week training course to be held annually in INCIENSA, Costa Rica. Seed funding was provided by the Overseas Development Agency, with the level of UK financial and technical support diminishing each year in the expectation that SIGLOS would become self-sustaining from fee income within three years. In the first year, scholarships for all participants were available with ODA funding. In the second and third years, one-third and then two-thirds of the participants had to be funded externally.

The aim of the project was to set up a sustainable health management and information systems training programme for middle-level health managers. It offered better access since costs are a mere fraction of the fees charged in Europe or North America. The course is taught in Spanish and employs the Action Learning approach.

Action learning (AL) is a combination of formal training with on-the-job problem solving. It is a relatively recent approach, becoming recognised in the mid-1970s, and has been described extensively by Reg Revans (Revans 1966, 1980, 1983). The learning equation presented by Revans (1987) shows how AL takes into account two starting points in the process of learning: 'being told by others' and 'finding out for ourselves'.

The first is called programmed instruction (P), and the second is questioning insight (Q). Learning is denoted by L and produces the learning equation: $L = P + Q$.

This represents the combination of P, which is in general the learning provided by traditional education and learning, and Q, which is largely the product of action learning.

AL in general involves training the participants in decision-making and action by getting them to solve spontaneous real-life problems, rather than allowing them to be passive recipients of someone else's wisdom and knowledge. The onus is on individual and teamwork development in here-and-now *real* situations. The application of this approach in the health sector is reported by Revans (1980).

Clutterbuck and Crainer (1991) described improvements achieved by Revans in NHS hospitals as exceptional, since he proved that health staff were able to identify their problems and find ways to solve them by working and learning from each other in real-life situations. Cassels and Janovsky (1991) have described a similar process for strengthening the management capacity of district and provincial health management teams clearly based on principles of AL.

The overall objective of the course is to develop the skills of middle-level managers in health institutions so that they can:

- analyse the community epidemiological health situation;
- identify and solve management issues at local level;
- produce strategic decisions;
- produce useful data presentation and communication;
- develop local and simple health information systems;
- design and conduct surveys at local level;

- use financial information;
- analyse data base information;
- use microcomputer technology.

Rapid changes in the region brought about through health sector reform programmes made it important to focus training efforts on those countries where new structures are permitting local managers greater control over resource allocation and programming. Also it afforded the opportunity to open manager's minds to new strategies designed to strengthen health systems.

Overview of the Three Evaluation Strategies

The evaluation strategies employed in this study are based on the framework developed by Kirkpatrick (1975). The conceptual framework presents four levels of evaluation (reaction, learning, behaviour and results) through key questions that should be answered by different means. Specific tools were designed for assessment at each level.

At the reaction level we attempted to discover the participants' opinions of the course, employing an 'end-of-course' questionnaire. The questionnaire remained unchanged over the three years. This information was used to improve the course for subsequent years. At the learning level we were concerned with measuring the acquisition through training of principles, facts and skills in order to assess how well participants had understood and absorbed the material. At the behaviour level we took attitudes as a proxy for behaviour. An attitude questionnaire was developed and used in a pre- and post-test design to assess the likely changes in management attitudes brought about by the course. This attitude questionnaire was modified each year.

The First Strategy: Year One

The first empirical evaluation design was agreed in the project proposal. It used a Kirkpatrick framework where follow-up data-collection was used to assess results and selected participants were given a grant to develop six carefully selected small projects in order to evaluate how they applied the skills learned. A follow-up questionnaire was sent, requesting any other evidence of the application of skills learnt at SIGLOS.

The Second Strategy: Year Two

The researcher focused on the identification of those who could benefit most from the course as well as searching for evidence of positive impact. It was decided to keep some of the evaluation elements agreed with the sponsors, such as the small projects grants. However, projects were not now granted a fixed sum per proposal, but financed according to the real cost of implementation.

The Third Strategy: Year Three

Blumenfeld and Holland (1971) stressed that any evaluation design without a pre-test and post-test will not generate evidence of behavioural change. Moreover a design without a control group will not generate evidence of the extent to which measured changes have been brought about by the training.

So the third strategy employed a group control according to the sample of participants selected for the evaluation study. It is an adaptation of the rigorous method reported by Taschereau (1998).

Each participant in the course and his/her homologue were asked to perform the same managerial task and the researcher analysed comparative performance, looking for differences that could be linked to the course. Case study analysis for each couple was applied.

Searching for Evidence of the Impact of SIGLOS-95 on the Performance of Health Service Managers

In this chapter only the third evaluation strategy is described. Management performance is difficult to define and measure. Although it is accepted that a good manager makes the best use of resources, it is arguable whether a good manager saves money within a budget or spends more than is budgeted for the sake of improving services. What is agreed is that a good manager is capable of producing satisfaction among clients through the services provided by his/her organisation.

However, even when measurement of nontechnical quality is possible, standard or baseline information is needed. Since standardised health care quality simply did not exist in Central American countries at the time of research, it was necessary to develop a baseline and measure improvements by comparing results.

Many factors could produce confusion, such as the cultural context of each participant, his private motivation and the local capacity (or lack of it) to produce any change. To avoid these wild-card variables, therefore, a control group was needed, individuals matched with each participant, each with a similar context and comparable situation to that being evaluated. In other words, a homologous manager should be found for each one in the sample. This new situation set the scene for a rigorous evaluation.

The following steps outline the methodology:

- participants for evaluation were selected according to changes in management attitudes during training;
- a homologue was selected for each participant. He was chosen for his similar experience and responsibilities in the health service but would have experienced no management training intervention;
- seven participants and their homologues signed contracts to take part in the privately conducted evaluation by an outside international consultancy. If the subsequent survey demonstrated improvement they would be paid an incentive sum;
- a baseline survey using exit interviews of patients was performed on each of the health facilities managed by the SIGLOS participants and those of the homologues. Participants might use the knowledge and skills learnt at SIGLOS to interpret the results of this first survey. Homologues might use their own experience, knowledge and skills.

The exit interviews on patients produced indicators of quality of care. The items in the questionnaire were based on a quality monitoring instrument developed by LSTM researchers in Ghana (Haran et al., 1993). On the basis of scores on these indicators the participants and their homologues were rated by independent raters for achievement of the training objectives. Table 11.1 summarises these results. This table gives the average score awarded to the two groups based on the following ratings: poor = 0 points; acceptable = 1 point; good = 2 points; very good = 3 points.

A simple analysis of results from the exit interviews at all the 14 facilities shows interesting differences in performance between SIGLOS trainees and the control group. Waiting time, for instance, is a variable that can be aggregated in terms of its statistical median. The differences between the sum of waiting times to see the doctor between the baseline survey and the evaluation survey can be taken as an estimation of the total time saved by both groups. Figure 11.1 illustrates how participants saved a total of 344 minutes from the median, while the homologues saved 220.

Table 11.1 Summary of mean ratings for participants and homologues

Aspect rated	Participants	Homologues
Ability to identify issues	1.57	1.29
Ability to produce strategic actions	1.86	1.43
Impact achieved	1.86	2.00
Overall assessment	1.57	1.71

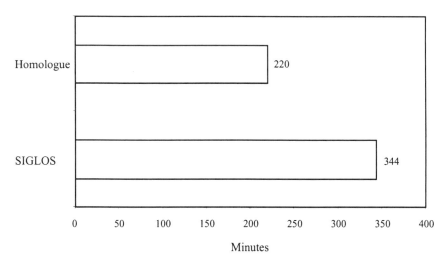

Figure 11.1 Total time saved (waiting time to see the doctor) by SIGLOS and homologue

Interpretation of this information has its limitations. However, it is important to point out that the managerial task produced improvements in such a critical issue as waiting time.

The analysis of key indicators of quality of medical care – such as whether a physical examination as performed – also shows a bigger pre-test to post-test improvement amongst the SIGLOS participants than in their homologues (see Figure 11.2).

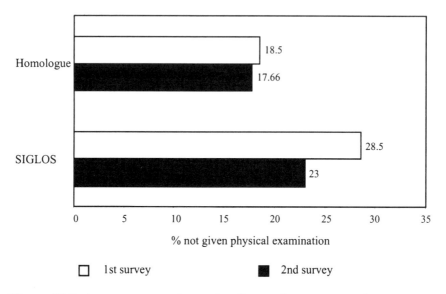

% not given physical examination

☐   1st survey   ■   2nd survey

**Figure 11.2 Average percentage of patients who were not given
             physical examinations**

Conclusions

Measuring the impact of a health management-training course is a task which
demands an holistic assessment. This would include the satisfaction and
reaction of participants to the training experience itself, participants' gains in
knowledge and skills and changes in attitudes and in behaviour. However, it
is recognised that even where training succeeds in producing desirable changes
among participants there is, sadly, no assurance that they will apply their new
knowledge, skills and attitudes to improve health services.

   Strategic follow-up methods rely entirely on the reaction of trainees such
subsequent assessment can be achieved by interviewing their managers,
supervisors and experts but it lacks facts in terms of performance and
improvements. Questionnaires and on-site interviews are major tools in this
kind of evaluation. Questionnaire surveys, however, sometimes suffer from
low response-rates, whilst interviews involve high cost and have a degree of
subjectivity in their analysis.

   It is hard to evaluate impact in situations where participants have different
professional backgrounds. It becomes even more complex if they belong to
different health institutions or systems and, if they come from different
countries, infinitely more difficult.

- A control group is one way of providing greater reliability in the assessment of the impact of health management training. In the absence of some kind of comparison group it could well be the participants' satisfaction, not the aims of training, that is being evaluated.
- Commissioning of small country projects to participants in training is an adventurous strategy. However, the danger is that the diversity of needs, local conditions and behaviour makes each comparison impossible.
- The results of this study suggest that quality assurance techniques to monitor health services from the client's perspective could be the most effective means of assessing management performance before and after training intervention. The investigation of this client perspective might be used to assess other types of intervention related to the improvement of health service initiative.
- Quality information is a very powerful management tool in identifying and solving local management problems. This information is most effectively obtained from exit interview surveys. In the majority of cases, this was the first time managers had monitored the performance of the health services they were responsible for.
- It was an innovative intervention for most and results were satisfactory. With few exceptions, managers were able to identify important problems affecting the quality of health services and develop means of solving them.
- Incentives, in the form of prizes and money, were a key to obtaining positive change. In real life there is sometimes no other way to produce improvements. Llewellyn reports that: 'Money is the most pervasive form of incentive in society, but economic rewards do give positive incentives towards productivity and they encourage clinicians to devote more time to direct patient care' (Llewellyn et al., 1999, p. 13).
- Health management training will have more impact if it were used to complement other policies, strategies and initiatives. More experience in impact evaluation is needed. The diversity of variables involved in measuring impact demands more research in developing practical approaches based on solid information.

References

Blumenfeld, W.S. and Holland, M.G. (1971), 'A Model for the Empirical Evaluation of Training Effectiveness', *Personnel Journal*, 50 (8), pp. 3–19.

Cassels, A. and Janovsky, K. (1991), *Strengthening Health Management in Districts and Provinces – Handbook for Facilitators*, WHO/SHS/DHS/91.3) WHO, Geneva.

Clutterbuck, D. and Crainer, S. (1991), *Los Maestros del Management: Hombres que llegaron mas lejos* Grijalbo, Barcelona.

Graig, R.L. (ed.) (1979), *Training and Development Handbook: A guide to human resource development* (2nd edn), McGraw-Hill, Wisconsin.

Haran, D., Iqbal, M. and Dovlo, D. (1993), 'Patients' Perceptions of the Quality of Care in Hospital Outpatient Departments: A quality assurance project in Eastern Region, Ghana. Quality and its applications', in J.F.L. Chan (ed.), *Papers from First Newcastle International Conference on Quality and Its Applications, 1–3 Sept, 1993*, University of Newcastle.

Hulme, D. (1990), *The Effectiveness of British Aid for Training, ActionAid Development Report* ActionAid, London.

Jones, M. and Mann, P. (1991), *HRD: International Perspective on Development and Learning*. Kurmanian Press Library of Management for Development, West Hartford, Conn.

Kerrigan, J.E. and Luke, J.S. (1987), *Management Training Strategies for Developing Countries* Lynne Rienner Publishers, Colorado.

Kirkpatrick, D.L. (1975), *Evaluating Training Programs*, American Society for Training and Development, Madison, Wisconsin.

Llewellyn, S., Eden, R. and Lay, C. (1999), *Financial and Professional incentives in Health Care: Comparing the UK and Canadian experiences International Journal of Public Sector Management* 12, 1, pp. 6–16.

Marsick, V. and O'Neil, J. (1999), 'The Many Faces of Action Learning', *Management Learning*, 30 (2), pp. 159–76.

Paul, S. (1983), *Training for Public Administration and Management in Developing Countries: A Review*, World Bank Working Papers No. 584, Management and Development Papers No 11, The World Bank, Washington.

Phillips, J.J. (1983), *Handbook of Training Evaluation and Measurement Methods*, Gulf Publishing Company, Houston.

Revans, R.W. (1966), *The Theory of Practice in Management*, MacDonald, London.

Revans, R.W. (1980), *Action Learning*, Blond and Briggs, London.

Revans, R.W. (1983), *The ABC of Action Learning*, Chartwell-Brant, Kent.

Revans, R.W. (1987), *International Perspectives on Action Learning: Manchester Training Handbook No 9*, Institute of Development Policy and Management, University of Manchester.

Rojas, Z., Sandiford, P. and Martinez, J. (1993), *Training Health Managers for Developing Countries in Developed Countries: Fish out of water?*, in M. Malek, J. Rasquinha, J and P. Vacani (eds), *Strategic Issues in Health Care Management*, John Wiley, Chichester, pp. 65–78.

Taschereau, S. (1998), *Evaluating the Impact of Training and Institutional Development Programmes*, Economic Development Institute of the World Bank, World Bank, Washington.

Tziner, A. and Haccoun, R. (1991), 'Personal and Situational Characteristics Influencing the Effectiveness of Transfer of Training Improvement Strategies', *Journal of Occupational Psychology*, 64, pp. 167–77.

SECTION FOUR
FUTURE TRENDS
IN DEVELOPMENT

Chapter Twelve

The Future of the European Health Sector – a Scenarios Approach

Leonard Lerer and John Kimberly

Introduction

In most European countries, governments, health service providers and organisations with an interest in health sector reform have engaged in a range of exercises to look at the future of health and health care. These initiatives included the gathering together of a range of experts and stakeholders, developing specific predictions and the design of policy and interventions. There has been much less work on the pan-European implications of transition in heath systems. In general, researchers are hampered by the paucity of fine-grained health economic data from the majority of European Union (EU) countries and by regional, social and cultural differences in the way that health services are financed and managed. While it is reasonable to expect growing standardisation across Europe associated with common reimbursement, a single currency and harmonisation of the pharmaceutical prices, the short-term view is one of fragmented health systems, increasing cost-containment pressures and growing controversy on the best-options for health service delivery.

Scenarios are an important method for dealing with uncertainty and rapid change (Schoemaker, 1995; Schwartz, 1991; Wack, 1985). Scenarios, futures and complex systems are increasingly being used as part of the strategic planning process as they have the potential for providing superb insights, building knowledge and nurturing vision. Scenarios are much more than simply a way of predicting the future, as they allow us to better understand the present, sensitise us to recognise change, and to enable us to respond more quickly and appropriately. Scenarios are less reassuring than conventional forecasts, but more challenging and therefore, more useful (Kahane, 1992). Scenarios can act as the 'wind tunnel' through which a course of action can be tested against possible, plausible futures.

Organisation Development in Health Care: Strategic Issues in Health Care Management, R.K. Rushmer, H.T.O. Davies, M. Tavakoli and M. Malek (eds), Ashgate Publishing Ltd, 2002.

We present a scenarios-based approach to the European health sector. The aim is to illustrate a robust and stimulating group-level analytical process to improve understanding of the implications of the complex interaction of key forces within the health sector, rather than to illustrate a single course of action. Our discussion and conclusions are loosely based on the key issues raised in the scenario exercise we describe, but essentially constitute the authors' view of the main forces driving and shaping transition in European health care. It is important to emphasise that the output is not a prediction about the future, but rather represents different options as to how current uncertainties may be better managed.

Methodology

Our approach to scenarios does not aim to build coherent, narrative pictures of the future, but rather to distil some important challenges through the juxtaposition of possible actions against possible trends (Leemhuis, 1985; Schaars, 1987). The scenario exercise thus aims to have a tangible and sustained linkage with the decision-making process in the health arena. In this chapter, we describe a 'typical' scenario exercise involving four groups of 6–8 participants (MBA candidates doing a health care management elective) conducted over a period of four weeks. During this period, the groups met collectively to review progress during four sessions lasting about 90 minutes and each group met individually for about four sessions lasting between one and two hours. The final scenarios were presented to, and discussed with, an audience, from the public and private health sector during a final session lasting about three hours.

In order to ensure that essential areas were covered, the groups were asked to develop their scenarios from specific perspectives – pharmaceuticals and biotechnology; information technology and the Internet; and health sector financing and health services. While imaginative thinking was encouraged, strict rules were followed as to the timetable and format of the outputs. The key steps were; the production of background material, description of the current situation, description of probable interventions, scenario development; testing of probable interventions against the scenarios and finally, producing a 'take-home' message (Figure 12.1).

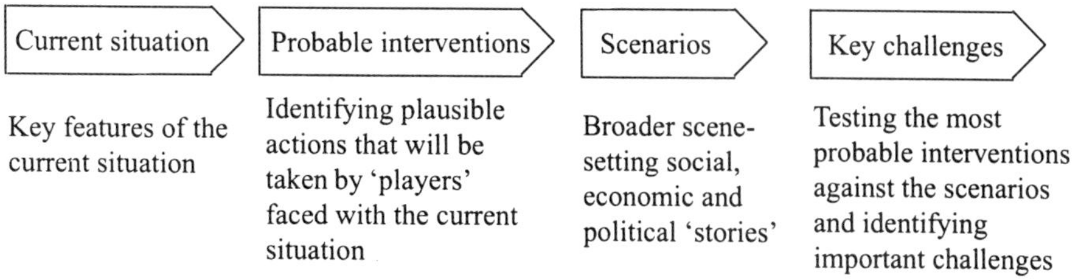

Current situation	Probable interventions	Scenarios	Key challenges
Key features of the current situation	Identifying plausible actions that will be taken by 'players' faced with the current situation	Broader scene-setting social, economic and political 'stories'	Testing the most probable interventions against the scenarios and identifying important challenges

Figure 12.1 The scenario process

Production of Background Material

The groups provided each other with a 'briefing pack' containing background on their specific areas of focus. The groups were encouraged to seek high quality material, rather than a large volume of documentation. Groups were not allowed to circulate more than three individual pieces of material (academic articles, websites or newspaper articles) and had to provide a single page summarising the essential points contained in the background material. The background material can also be provided in the form of research papers especially written for the scenario group. The aim of the background material is to enrich the debate and should thus focus on current controversies and important concerns.

Description of the Current Situation

Using three brief points, groups were asked to describe the current situation pertaining to their particular areas of focus. The purpose was to identify the most important features of the current situation and potential sources of conflict or issues responsible for substantial conflict and controversy.

Description of the Probable Interventions

Using two brief points, the groups described, what they predicted to be the most likely actions that government and the private sector would consider or take, when faced with the 'current situation'. The probable interventions were an attempt to rapidly make a best prediction, which would be tested and then fine-tuned during the scenario exercise.

Scenario Development

Groups provided two brief stories about the future of Europe. The stories had to be reasonably plausible, rational tales of the social, political, economic and technological environment in Europe within a 5–10 year time-horizon. The stories were deliberately devoid of any health-related content. The groups were discouraged from developing scenarios that represented diametrically opposed world-views, such as war versus peace or affluence versus poverty.

Testing Probable Interventions against the Scenarios

Using a simple matrix, the key challenges emanating from each intervention in each scenario were identified. This served as the foundation for discussion and identification of the current leading indicators of long-term trends in the health sector.

Results

The Current Situation

European health care systems are under increasing pressure due to new, costly technologies and growing public demand for improved services. The market for pharmaceutical products is growing to cater for an ageing and more affluent population. The introduction of therapeutic 'niches' or designer drugs, lifestyle drugs and gene-based therapeutics results in increases in public sector health spending, which continues to be a controversial political issue. European health care is fragmented with each country pursuing a different strategy and potential exists to reduce inefficiencies and improve communications. There is increasing pressure to narrow the disparities in price and services between European countries and to have an EU-wide standard for health service provision.

Probable Interventions

Faced with transition, each component of the health sector will take a particular course of action. Pharmaceutical companies will increasingly use direct-to-consumer advertising and other marketing tools to increase demand for sophisticated and expensive drugs. The European Commission will increasingly exercise its mandate as a standardising body for health services. The aims of this standardisation will include uniformity in quality, and the types and intensity of interventions. A free-market framework (roughly akin to the Clinton's managed competition) will be introduced. The private sector will increasingly play a role in improving connectivity and efficiency in European health care systems. European patients will demand more access to health information and personal health records, forcing increased disclosure and transparency, especially from hospitals and insurers. Patients will become more vocal and more mobile, seeking care outside their home countries and forcing national insurers to pay. Governments, reluctant to undertake any politically dangerous, radical supply-side health sector reforms will encourage the sale of complementary health insurance, thereby attempting to transfer some of the health cost burden onto consumers.

Scenario Development

Two sets of scenarios (illustrated in Tables 12.1 and 12.2) represent underlying themes across the social, economic and political arenas. Europe faces the challenge of managing growing consumer spending and rapid technological advances. Political changes, such as conservatism, may make it difficult to reduce disparities in economic development between EU countries and to integrate the former socialist countries of Eastern Europe. The rise of a consumer society, widening gaps between the rich and the poor, and the loss of social capital may accelerate the erosion of national and EU-wide solidarity. In this environment, the private sector may increasingly enter into areas and service provision traditionally controlled by the state. A pervasive theme in the scenarios is the impact of technology on the public sector, business and the individual. The Internet and mobile telephony are seen as vehicles to allow Europe to 'leapfrog' ahead of the USA in the creation of a technologically advanced society.

Testing Probable Interventions against the Scenarios

Examples of the key challenges matrix are provided in Tables 12.3 and 12.4. The need to develop innovative approaches to stem the demand for expensive treatments that only marginally improve outcome, and to deal with the impacts of improved diagnostics and genomics, is highlighted. A common thread in the matrices is the prospect of increased segmentation of the market for health and health services across Europe. Variations based on disease, age and ability

Table 12.1   Two scenarios focusing on consumers and politics

European renaissance	Shift to the right
The EMU's success leads to increased pan-European competition and consolidation of industries	Although slowing the trend towards the ageing of the population in member states, increased immigration fuels nationalism
Economic growth in Europe increases consumer spending and government revenues	Rich EU member states are reluctant to fund EU-wide projects and transfer payments
Consumers are empowered by technological advances, including information access via the Internet	Because of the changing geopolitical environment, member states shift spending towards defence

Table 12.2   Two scenarios focusing on economics and technology

Privatisation	Technology
Member countries come under increasing pressure from the EU to stay within strict public sector budgets. Power in many areas of policy shifts to Brussels. Budget cuts in governmental spending across Europe lead to increasing investment from the private sector in areas traditionally controlled by the state	Information and other technologies continue to have a pervasive effect across many areas of public and private life. Over and above simply automating existing processes, these developments begin to change traditional business models, especially in the service industries

to pay will allow providers and pharmaceutical companies to extract more value from patient or consumer relationships, and introduces the prospect of an increasing number of direct financial transactions between providers and patients. The EU regulatory framework will struggle to keep pace with, and shape, the evolving health care market, especially in areas such as the internet, consumer or patient protection, and the management of therapeutic technologies including pharmaceuticals. Setting normative standards and improving services will be particularly difficult in the light of pressures on public sector spending. Private companies will desire a larger share of the European health space and governments may increasingly hand over various functions to the private sector. The power of insurance companies, managed care providers, physician group practices and pharmaceutical companies may increase in a 'fragmented' Europe.

Table 12.3   Key challenges matrix focusing on health care financing

	Scenario 1 European renaissance	Scenario 2 Shift to the right
Intervention 1 Substantial commitment from all governments to establish a harmonised European health care system	The EU regulatory framework struggles to keep up with consumer demand driven by rapidly evolving consumer technology. Robust revenues reduce government incentives to reform the health system and improve efficiency	The underfunded European health care system struggles to sustain support from member states. Member states have difficulty defining the level of universal coverage and preventing unequal access
Intervention 2 Governments privatise health service provision in order to increase efficiency	Reduced bargaining power vis-à-vis the large, consolidated service providers diminishes quality of service	Because health care is not the top priority, government regulation of the market is loose resulting in 'cherry picking' by privatised providers

Table 12.4   Key challenges matrix focusing on health services

	Scenario 1 Privatisation	Scenario 2 Technology
Intervention 1 EU initiatives to ensure that increased access to information	Need to cope with increasingly complex data protection issues as well as targeted, possibly unethical, advertising. In addition, the issue of rationing becomes increasingly important as cutbacks occur in certain unprofitable sectors	Challenge of coping with increased demand from patients for expensive new treatments. Also need to deal with the frustration that arises from knowledge of new treatments that are not available in a particular health care system
Intervention 2 Regulatory reform to facilitate easier mobility of European patents	Geographic consolidation of speciality centres will make access difficult for some patients. The main challenge facing health care companies will be managing their businesses across a range of health care systems	As a result of increased cross border mobility there will be an increase in demand for certain technologies that are available in only certain geographic locations. The challenge is going to be to manage the cost to the payers and the demand for this technology at the centres themselves

Discussion

We have presented some of the common themes identified during a health scenarios exercise. The consumer or patient will increasingly becoming the focal point of private sector health activity and marketing. Pharmaceutical manufacturers will use every possible means to directly market sophisticated and expensive treatment within an affluent, ageing market of consumers with complementary health insurance. As governments become increasingly marginalised in the health transaction, it is likely that we will see increased controversy over consumer protection, privacy and intellectual property. The growth of a pan-European health industry is inevitable, as barriers to doing business fall. We are already seeing evidence of consolidation in the pharmaceutical industry and vertical integration, with the disappearance of wholesalers, pressure on retail pharmacies and nascent pharmaceutical benefit management (PBM) structures.

The pervasive influence of the internet and new technologies is challenging existing legal, social and business paradigms in health. The diffusion of e-health innovation from the USA to Europe is substantially influenced by the differences between private and social insurance-based health systems. The connectivity or integration model (linking multiple providers, payers and consumers) is at the heart of the US e-health model. The fact that a country such as France has provided almost all its citizens with a smart-card to facilitate all health related transactions, indicates that there may be little potential for USA-style connectivity solutions in Europe. Similarly, the way that care is delivered, physician–patient interaction and the concentration of specialist care in state-funded institutions make it likely that the strong consumer focus of US e-health offerings will have to be considerably modified for application within the EU. Notwithstanding the cultural, regulatory, political and economic constraints, it is not unreasonable to predict that e-health solutions will become increasingly important as health service delivery tools in Europe, especially as mobile internet applications become part of everyday life.

Health and health sector reform is a political issue and the inability to comprehensively overhaul and standardise health services has long-term consequences for individual governments and the EU as a whole. The role of the European Commission and individual states is characterised by the waxing and waning of power and influence amongst the players. We need to be constantly aware of the dangers of a short-term, country-specific, politically expedient approach to health sector reform that could hamper progress towards a more equitable and efficient pan-European health system.

Conclusion

Scenario building has also come to be regarded by some, as an irrelevant, time-consuming exercise. We believe that this criticism may be, in part, justified by the false belief that scenarios can provide 'black or white' policy answers. We use scenarios to grapple with complexity. We cannot predict the future accurately, no matter how well we know the past and present. However, if we start thinking about complexity, we start to see patterns emerging from the chaos (Senge, 1990; Brown and Eisenhardt, 1998). At the beginning of the twenty-first century, there are widespread differences in the way that health care is perceived and delivered in Europe. While it may be optimistic to predict a rapid convergence in health regulation and financing, it is clear that some strong drivers of change beginning to manifest. These include legal challenges for reimbursement for cross-border care, the single currency and the growth of e-health.

The European health space is certainly in a state of change, and innovative tools, such as scenarios, may improve our understanding of the drivers of this change. It always remains difficult to link thinking about health sector reform to appropriate action, but we need to use every means at our disposal to be in a position to detect emerging trends and better discern the direction of the 'winds of change' in the health sector.

References

Brown, S.L. and Eisenhardt, K.M. (1998), *Competing on the Edge – Strategy as Structured Chaos*, Harvard Business School Press, Cambridge, Mass.

Kahane, A. (1992), 'Scenarios for Energy: Sustainable world vs global mercantilism', *Long Range Planning*, 25(4), pp. 38–46.

Leemhuis, J.P. (1985), 'Using Scenarios to Develop Strategies', *Long Range Planning*, 18(2), pp. 30–7.

Schaars, S.P. (1987), 'How to Develop and Use Scenarios.' *Long range Planning*, 20(1), pp. 21–9.

Schoemaker, P. (1995), 'Scenario Planning: A tool for strategic thinking', *Sloan Management Review*, pp. 25–40.

Schwartz, P. (1991), *The Art of the Long View: Planning for the future in an uncertain world*, Doubleday, New York.

Senge, P. (1990), *The Fifth Discipline*, Doubleday, New York.

Wack, P. (1985), 'Scenarios: Uncharted waters ahead', *Harvard Business Review* (Sept./Oct.), pp. 73–89.

Chapter Thirteen

Institutional Change and Trust in the National Health Service: Examining the Impact of Reform on the NHS Value Structure

Steven Simoens and Robert McMaster

Introduction

Since its inception, the UK's National Health Service has gone through prolonged periods of institutional change. Most recently, the 1989 and 1997 reforms (Secretary of State for Health, 1989, 1997) have introduced a variety of new organisational structures in the health service. To date, the majority of evaluatory studies have focused on the consequences of the 1989 and 1997 reform packages for efficiency, equity, quality, consumer choice, and responsiveness. Much less attention has been devoted to the potential impact of institutional change on the nature of relationships between stakeholders of the NHS. This chapter provides an initial exploration of how the 1989 and 1997 legislation affected the belief and value structure underlying the pre-1989 NHS and how it contributed to the erosion of trust in and within the health service.

Our interest in the consequences of institutional change for trust has been stimulated by recent work which regards trust as a potential source of enhanced economic performance (see, for instance, Arrighetti et al., 1997). Such a link would suggest that any erosion of trust induced by the 1989 and 1997 legislation is likely to adversely affect the narrow efficiency targets sought by the previous and current government. This is a much neglected side effect of the reforms and is in stark contrast with the projected cost savings of £1 billion as reported in the 1997 White Paper *The New NHS: Modern, dependable* (Secretary of State for Health, 1997).

Organisation Development in Health Care: Strategic Issues in Health Care Management, R.K. Rushmer, H.T.O. Davies, M. Tavakoli and M. Malek (eds), Ashgate Publishing Ltd, 2002.

The chapter initially outlines the concept of trust and reviews and comments upon economic, sociological and institutional approaches to trust. The health service reforms of 1989 and 1997 are described and the possible implications of these changes for the degree of entrustment between the various stakeholders of the NHS are explored. The chapter specifically focuses on the impact of institutional change on three relationships: between purchasers and providers, between clinicians and patients, and between clinicians and NHS management. Finally, a different perspective on the 1989 and 1997 reforms is presented.

Definition of Trust

Famously, Arrow called on analysts to recognise trust as both a necessary and sufficient condition for economic activity. He emphasised that 'virtually every transaction has within itself an element of trust, certainly any commercial transaction conducted over a period of time' (Arrow 1975, p. 23). Despite Arrow's attempt to map out the impact of trust on economic development and performance, he was less successful in fashioning a robust definition.

Gambetta (1998, p. 6) provides a definition of trust that is framed in principal-agent theory:

> trust is a particular level of subjective probability with which an agent assesses that another agent or group of agents will perform a particular action, both before he can monitor such action and in a context in which it affects his own action.

Trust as defined by Gambetta has no normative properties in contrast with the everyday use of the word. It just refers to some degree of reliability or predictability of the agent's behaviour and to trust implies some diminution in behavioural uncertainty (Zucker, 1986).

In this respect, Sako's (1992) delineation of trust which reflects different types of behavioural risk in commercial contracting should be noted. He distinguished between three different types of trust in exchange relationships: contractual trust, where a party is trusted to adhere to the terms of the agreement, competence trust, that is the belief in a party's ability to provide commodities of a specified quality, and goodwill trust, which pertains to the extent to which a party can go beyond mere fulfilment of her/his tasks to taking new initiatives for mutual benefit without seeking undue personal advantage.

In health care, trust is likely to play a role in three relationships: between purchasers and providers in the NHS, between clinicians and patients and between clinicians and NHS management. Given the fundamental uncertainty about the incidence and severity of illness in the population and the uncertain effect of health care on health status, patients and managers have to rely on the judgement and clinical expertise of clinicians to provide care in the best interests of the patient and the NHS. Due to the difficulties involved in accurately measuring and predicting the range, volume, price and quality of health care services to be provided, contracts between purchasers and providers will necessarily be incomplete. In the presence of information asymmetry between parties, trust allows parties to cope with environmental uncertainty by reducing behavioural uncertainty. For instance, GPs can more easily deal with unpredicted fluctuations in demand by orienting their actions on the basis of the expected behaviour of NHS Trusts.

Theories of Trust

This section briefly describes and criticises different approaches to trust. More specifically, the calculative, self-interested trust of mainstream economics is contrasted with the socially-embedded trust of anthropology, sociology and heterodox economic approaches.

Conventional economists tend to encapsulate trust in a rational choice framework and conjecture that parties are motivated to trust for calculated, self-interested reasons. Trust in this context follows directly from the economic assumptions of rational utility maximisation (Fisman and Khanna, 1999). The interest in trust in economics has mainly come from two perspectives: transaction cost economics and game theory.

In transaction cost economics, the concept of trust is generally discarded in favour of the notion of opportunism, that is self-interest-seeking with guile. Williamson even goes so far as to say that 'the study of economic organization is better served by treating commercial contracts without reference to trust' (Williamson, 1993, p. 99). Under conditions of bounded rationality, asset specificity, uncertainty, complexity, frequency and small-numbers bargaining, parties may engage in post-contractual opportunistic behaviour and extract concessions from the other party. Consequently, trade would be severely impaired without recourse to appropriate enforcement mechanisms to attenuate the occurrence of opportunism. Following Williamson, trust is regarded as an insufficient safeguard against opportunism and parties should instead rely on other governance structures such as vertical integration and long-term contracts (Williamson, 1985).

However, by presuming that opportunism is innate human behaviour, Williamson fails to fully appreciate the potential of trust as a governance structure. First, the establishment of a relationship based on trust may allow parties to economise on transaction costs, both *ex ante* and *ex post*. Ex ante transaction costs refer to the costs of writing and negotiating an agreement. Ex post transaction costs refer to the costs of enforcing, monitoring and, possibly, renegotiating contracts. Professional associations such as the British Medical Association and Royal Colleges effectively reduce costs to the NHS of monitoring professional behaviour through, for instance, peer review and ethical codes (Croxson, 1999).

Second, game theory recognises the importance of trust as rational self-interested behaviour in long-term relationships. Repetition makes parties realise that rivalrous behaviour in the short run could impair the sustenance of cooperation and undermine mutual long-term benefit flows. Therefore, the desire to safeguard a reputation of trustworthiness may act as a constraint on opportunism.

As opposed to the Williamsonian *homo economicus* who is purposefully calculative, sociological theories focus on the social mechanisms that foster trust and that provide a rich variety of enforcement mechanisms. The reductionist perspective of human behaviour adopted by conventional economists is replaced by the notion of socially-embedded trust that is the product of either affectual, traditional or value-rational behaviour (Lyons and Mehta, 1997a, b). Affectual behaviour refers to personal trust relationships built on feelings of friendship and even devotion to the exchange party. Traditional behaviour becomes manifest in the adherence of parties to routines or customary practices. Value-rational behaviour reflects the commitment of parties to the same belief system and to shared values. North (1990) points out that trust engendered by any of these types of behaviour may help to resolve ubiquitous agency problems.

However, both economic and sociological approaches marginalise the role of institutional normative structures in creating and sustaining trust. Williamson, for instance, fails to appreciate the influence of the institutional environment which, in his analysis, 'is mainly taken as exogenous' (Williamson 1993, p. 43). In general, three institutions can be identified that act as a vehicle for trust production: the legal system, professional associations, and technical standards (Deakin et al., 1997). Arrighetti et al. (1997) argued that institutional trust can play an important role in promoting stability, especially in intra-organisational interactions, in offsetting asymmetries of power between parties, and in decreasing uncertainty.

The 1989 NHS Reforms

Prior to the 1989 reforms, District Health Authorities exercised the joint responsibility of planning health care services and managing the providers of these services, i.e. hospitals. The previous government's legislation, *Working for Patients* (Secretary of State for Health, 1989), radically altered this organisational structure by introducing market-oriented interactions between parties in the health service and by imposing a contractual relationship between different bodies in the NHS. The centrepiece of the reforms was the division between purchasers and providers, and the devolution of budgetary responsibility from Health Authorities.

On the purchaser side, District Health Authorities were expected to reduce their role in providing health care and to move towards a commissioning role. In addition, GPs could opt to become fundholders and hold a budget to purchase a limited range of hospital services for their patients. District Health Authorities continued to purchase services for those GPs who did not elect to become GP fundholders and for those services that did not fall under the responsibility of GP fundholders. On the provider side, hospitals could gain independence from their Health Authority by becoming NHS Trusts. Hospitals that did not obtain Trust status remained under the management of the Health Authority.

The separation of functions and the devolution of budgetary responsibility was intended to stimulate competitive pressures at both primary and secondary care levels, and in this manner enhance cost awareness, whilst simultaneously improving the quality, if not the equity, of care (Chalkley and Malcolmson, 1996; Flynn and Williams, 1997). This reform package represented a considerable shift in the culture of NHS activities (Flynn and Williams, 1997; Hughes et al., 1997; Montgomery, 1997). Contracting formalised relationships between actors across the purchaser-provider split. Communication between parties was inevitably drawn into recognised channels, as opposed to informal arrangements. However, contracts in the internal market carried no legal recognition. Thus, whilst the shift to contracting is clearly a market-oriented alignment, it does not represent full-scale privatisation in that contracting parties do not possess the property rights to seek judicial arbitration and are subject to NHS Executive guidance. Consequently, Montgomery (1997) argued that the 1989 reforms are better interpreted as a means of performance management.

The 1997 NHS Reforms

The current government claimed to be committed to abandoning the internal market for health care. Certainly, the White Paper *The New NHS: Modern, dependable* (Secretary of State for Health, 1997), emphasises integrated care and cooperation as opposed to the competitive imperative previously sought, but seldom attained. Working with Health Authorities, primary care groups and clinicians from NHS Trusts are to take the lead in planning the local patterns of service provision within the three-year Health Improvement Programme. This trilateral arrangement envisages Health Authorities to act in a regulatory capacity, and primary care groups and NHS Trusts to work in partnership.

The reorganisation further empowers GPs, despite the cessation of GP fundholding. New, larger primary care groups are established consisting of all GPs in a local area together with community nurses. Over time, these primary care groups can become freestanding primary care Trusts, which hold a unified group budget covering general medical services, hospital and community health services, and prescribing. Within the context of this new, collaborative approach, primary care groups will agree long-term service agreements with NHS Trusts.

Nevertheless, there are aspects of the 1997 reforms that suggest that not only has the internal market apparatus not entirely been abandoned, it has also been reinforced in some respects. Witness, for instance, the retention of the purchaser-provider split, the persistence of contracting interfaces, and the further devolution of budgetary responsibility.

By separating the planning of secondary care, as articulated through the commissioning process, from its provision, the 1997 legislation not only retains the integral structure of the internal market, but also the divergence of incentives to agents within it. Even in an atmosphere of cooperation, the flow of funds from primary care groups to secondary care providers will at least be influenced by considerations of appropriation. Moreover, the reform package stresses the importance of decentralised management, characteristic of other market-oriented initiatives of the previous government, and places great emphasis on devolved budgeting (Montgomery, 1997).

The Pre-1989 NHS and its Foundation upon Trust

The pre-1989 NHS operated on a basis of high value congruence. Given that the underlying value structure in the NHS was governed by the Hippocratic ethos, health care providers were viewed as sharing a common set of values based upon professional ethics and caring (Robinson and Le Grand, 1994). Barker et al. (1997) contended that common ownership across any exchange interface within the NHS implied that actors were likely to share objectives rather than pursue independent and conflicting goals. The adherence to a common belief system and behavioural patterns consistent with the prevailing culture in the health service established and sustained high levels of trust in and within the NHS.

Prior to the 1989 reforms, the NHS was characterised by a high degree of clinician autonomy (Klein, 1995). Clinicians retained ultimate authority over the allocation of resources and the provision of services, usually based on professionally defined criteria of need. This injected a considerable degree of goodwill trust in the relationship between clinician and patient, and supported the expectation that the clinician's actions were solely guided by the patient's interests.

Public trust in the NHS was reinforced by the ability of clinicians to provide high-quality care. Professional organisations enforced high standards of medical and postgraduate education and controlled entry into the profession. Competence trust was (and still is) invested in physicians and other clinical staff by means of the professional code of practice of clinicians and training accreditation as ratified by the Royal Colleges. Montgomery (1997) further indicated that the NHS prior to the 1990 reforms had an array of quality control mechanisms, ranging from the Audit Commission to community health councils.

The dominance of the clinical profession and the prevailing Hippocratic ethos, however, were accompanied by considerable performance ambiguity and actor discretion. In addition, professional accreditation was viewed as a constraint on the market mechanism – analogous to an entry barrier that inflates costs – by encouraging the potential pursuit of 'Rolls Royce' service standards without any awareness of costs.

This perception of a lack of accountability shaped certain aspects of the 1989 reforms. First, the pre-1989 NHS exhibited too much entrustment in the ability and incentives of clinicians. The absence of a robust evaluatory framework provided clinicians with the opportunity to free ride. Second, the extensive degree of entrustment invested in clinicians did not contribute to allocative efficiency.

By introducing more market traits in the NHS, accountability and efficiency were expected to be enhanced. As Keaney and Lorimer (1999) noted, such an interpretation of the 1989 reforms is predicated on a rather weak neoclassical analysis, which does not take account of knowledge gaps and which assumes that patients are sovereign consumers. Moreover, the ramifications of these reforms on the role of trust within the NHS received no attention in the government's legislation.

The 1990 NHS Reforms and the Erosion of Trust

The 1989 reforms introduced specifically market-oriented mechanisms into both the allocation of resources and the organisation of the NHS. These reforms represented significant institutional change and, obviously, the patterns and extent of trust between parties cannot be isolated from such change. Yet there is little direct empirical evidence tracing out the nature of this change and how it impacts on the ability of the health service to meet its ultimate objectives.

The internal market was based on the assumption that allowing purchasers to switch contracts between rival providers creates efficiency gains in the provision of health care. The message implicit in the 1989 legislation was that the health care sector could be regarded as a market place and that health care resembled other commodities. Although the previous government presented the reforms as a continuing evolution of, rather than a breach with, the fundamental principles of the NHS, the introduction of the internal market represented a significant change in how health care professionals and the public thought about health care.

It is argued that the government's legislation resulted in a deterioration in the degree of entrustment because of the scope for potential conflict between the established egalitarian and Hippocratic ethos of the pre-1989 NHS and the value structure associated with a more market aligned incentive structure introduced by the 1989 reforms. Three factors contributed to the erosion of trust in the post-1989 NHS: the prominent role of managers in the health service, the implementation of an evaluatory framework for assessing performance, and the introduction of contractual relationships between purchasers and providers.

The division between planning and delivery created by the 1989 legislation combined with a prominent role for the NHS Executive in setting contract guidelines and regulating the conduct of purchasers and providers increased the role of managers in the health service. The 1989 reforms further supported the shift towards a managerialistic NHS – initiated by the Griffiths Report in 1983 (DHSS, 1983) – in which decisions about the organisation and provision of health care were increasingly made by individuals whose background in medicine was limited. This process was compounded by the recruitment policy of managers. NHS Trusts were encouraged to actively recruit managers with private sector experience and to further their positions of responsibility. Again, this can be interpreted as a weakening in the Hippocratic ethos as the dominant value structure. The external recruitment of managers with little previous knowledge of the pre-1989 health service implied that such staff was less influenced by, and more detached from the prevailing value structure.

An evaluatory framework was set up in response to the lack of accountability that characterised the pre-1989 NHS. The 1989 legislation created an additional body, the Clinical Standards Advisory Group, to oversee standards of care, access to, and availability of services. The role of management was expanded through the deployment of the purchaser efficiency index as an evaluatory benchmark for relative performance. This acted as a limited constraint on the discretion of clinicians in that NHS Trust performance was (partially) judged on the throughput of patients. NHS Trust managers could legitimately insist that managers adopt practices that were conducive to increasing the number of consultant episodes. This adjusted the relative position of NHS managers and clinicians in favour of the former.

The division between purchasers and providers and the emphasis on contractual relationships may have contributed to a decline in goodwill and contract trust. By superimposing potentially conflicting values, the nature of interaction changes and purchasers and providers become less inclined to reciprocate shared values in an informal manner. The very nature of any sort of contractual relationship implies that parties extract different benefit flows (Macneil, 1981). Although parties may not be entirely disengaged from shared beliefs, the pattern of expressing those beliefs has been radically altered. Flynn et al. (1997) examined the particular features of community health services and found evidence that District Health Authority purchasers expressed their commitment to developing collaborative relationships with providers, but in bargaining and negotiations over financial resources frequently engaged in adversarial behaviour.

Studies into the process of contracting in the NHS have documented the rising importance of the language and style of corporate activity in UK hospitals (Hughes et al., 1997; McHale et al., 1997; Kitchener ,1998). Moreover, Hughes et al. (1997) and Kitchener (1998) traced instances of considerable deteriorations in the relationships between contracting parties (usually NHS Trusts and contracting Health Authorities). Both studies illustrated that disputes were more likely to arise where a more formal contracting frame was adopted. In one study on contracting policies adopted by Welsh Health Authorities and

NHS Trusts (Hughes et al., 1997), instances were identified where central authority had to be exerted to resolve disputes.

Although the introduction of contractual relationships may have engendered a diminution in the level of trust between the internal actors in the NHS, the magnitude of any such erosion of trust is likely to have been constrained by the specific nature of NHS contracts. Contracts between purchasers and providers are not legally enforceable. This implies that the contracting process in the NHS had to rely on other aspects of the contractual environment, such as trust, routines and cultural factors (Goddard and Mannion, 1998). Therefore, the value structure that prevailed in the NHS prior to 1989 still played a significant role in governing relationships between parties in the internal market.

GP fundholding, introduced by the 1989 legislation, illustrates the incursion by a more cost-conscious belief structure and the resulting erosion of trust. The motives and decisions of such organisations can be questioned given that the incentives to physicians embodied by GP fundholding potentially threaten the credibility of the GP's role as the patient's agent. In particular, the GP's increased budgetary responsibility alters his or her decision making frame and may create a conflict between the clinician's interests and the patient's interests. For instance, Glennerster et al. (1994) showed how the GP fundholding scheme included financial incentives for GPs to indulge in 'cream skimming', that is to remove patients with expensive health care needs from their lists.

Moreover, public trust in the health service may suffer when different arrangements for organising and financing care are perceived to influence the provision of health care. The GP fundholding scheme has been accused of introducing a 'two-tier system', i.e. to offer better access to hospital care for patients registered with fundholding practices compared with those registered with non-fundholding practices, regardless of need (Dixon and Glennerster, 1995). A related concern was the perceived inequality in funding arising from the various financial incentives offered to fundholding practices (Robinson and Hayter, 1995). Such claims are likely to diminish popular trust in the egalitarian and Hippocratic ethos of the NHS.

In effect, the internal market may have produced counterproductive results by inducing agency type problems between managers and clinicians, between clinicians and patients, and between purchasers and providers. The resulting behavioural and environmental uncertainty may, ultimately, adversely affect the narrow efficiency targets sought by the previous government.

The 1997 NHS Reforms: the Restoration of Trust?

The question can be raised as to whether the 1997 reforms will redress any trust deterioration induced by the 1989 legislation. Trust received little attention in the government's White Papers (Secretary of State for Health, 1997). The promotion of trust between parties in the NHS may thus be considered not to be a priority of the 1997 reform package.

At the moment, the question remains open. On the one hand, the government's emphasis on relational contracting models and the proposed shift away from competitive relations and annual contracts towards collaborative partnerships and long-term agreements (Goddard and Mannion, 1998), are likely to provide a basis for fostering both contract and goodwill trust. Moreover, the inclusion of representatives from the local community in the boards of primary care groups and NHS Trusts, the requirement that NHS Trusts hold their meeting in public, and the development of a new NHS Patient's Charter may go some way to restoring popular trust in the health service.

On the other hand, despite the rhetoric of the government, the current reform package retains – and in some instances even strengthens – the central elements of the 1989 reforms. First, the 1997 reforms devolve even more budgetary responsibility to the successors of GP fundholders, i.e. primary care groups and primary care Trusts. Second, the imposition of further dimensions in the evaluatory framework through the creation of two NHS watchdogs – the National Institute for Clinical Excellence and the Commission for Health Improvement – may be the source of tension: will the formalised monitoring of clinical activities make health care professionals more accountable, or more resistant to the implementation of the government's legislation?

The only safe conclusion to draw is that it appears that the current government has not fully appreciated the potential importance of trust within a complex organisational system, such as the NHS, and is as culpable as many conventional economists in not grasping how institutional change affects the degree of entrustment between parties in the NHS.

A Different Perspective on the 1989 and 1997 Reforms

The discussion so far has concentrated on the impact of institutional reform on the value structure underlying the NHS. To that effect, the implications of some of the policy changes as introduced by the 1989 and 1997 reforms on the economic relationships between NHS stakeholders were explored. The relationship between institutional change and trust in the NHS can also be addressed from a different angle, namely, how can institutional reform be used as an instrument to promote a new value structure, in the case that such a change in values is needed.

Arguably, the NHS was created in order to impose a new set of values upon the medical profession. One of the founding principles of the NHS is its concern with the health of the total population irrespective of willingness or ability to pay. In order to achieve this goal and to maximise population health subject to a budget constraint, it has become necessary not simply to provide those services that are effective, but to carry out only those procedures that are cost-effective. This change in the culture of delivering health care masks a conflict of interest between agents and principals: the official ethos of the medical profession which is based on the paradigm of effectiveness clashes with the public interest which demands the delivery of cost-effective services. During this transitional period, the behaviour of clinicians is likely to become less predictable and, as a consequence, trust is eroded.

If the medical profession cannot be relied upon to pursue only cost-effective medicine, institutional reform may serve to create the appropriate incentive structure to bring about the required culture change. Therefore, the 1989 and 1997 reforms can be regarded to have facilitated the transition towards the cost-effectiveness paradigm by imposing a more market-aligned incentive structure on the medical profession. This also implies that the calculative, self-interested trust of mainstream economics acts as an interim arrangement until the medical profession and the public share the same values and it can be replaced by the socially-embedded trust of anthropology, sociology, and heterodox economic approaches.

Conclusion

The creation of an 'internal market' has led to some erosion of trust between the stakeholders of the NHS. Although a new, more market aligned incentive structure has been superimposed on the Hippocratic ethos that governed the pre-1989 NHS, the new value structure has not entirely replaced the old culture. Therefore, economic relationships in the post-1997 NHS are likely to be characterised by a mixture of the socially-embedded trust of sociology and the calculative self-interested trust of mainstream economics.

The importance of trust and entrustment in and within the NHS is an underdeveloped area of research. Hence, it is difficult to gauge the impact of diminished trust between parties on the ability of the NHS to meet its hybrid objectives. The Hippocratic ethos underpinning clinical activity may be insulated from any climatical change in the degree of trust between actors in the new organisational structure. However, there may be an indirect qualitative influence on the ability and motivation of staff to perform their tasks effectively. There is no doubt that the 1989 reforms introduced more rigidities, via the contracting process, into the health service. At the same time, it did pose clinicians with important questions as to the cost-effectiveness of many treatment methods, although perhaps in a rather alien fashion that engendered resistance and distaste.

Any further research by policy makers and economists should focus on the potential role of trust in general, and with respect to the provision of health care in particular. The unique nature of the NHS presents an opportunity for redressing this oversight. Moreover, attention should be paid to the impact of trust on NHS performance. Finally, identifying and developing new structures and practices that enhance the public credibility of the NHS and that foster trust between the internal actors of the NHS is an important avenue of future research.

Acknowledgements

The authors would like to thank Alan Williams for comments on earlier drafts of this chapter. HERU is funded by the Chief Scientist Office of the Scottish Executive Health Department (SEHD). The views expressed in this chapter are those of the authors and not SEHD.

References

Arrighetti, A., Bachmann, R. and Deakin, S. (1997), 'Contract Law, Social Norms and Inter-firm Cooperation', *Cambridge Journal of Economics*, 21, pp. 171–95.

Arrow, K.J. (1975), 'Gifts and Exchanges', in E.S. Phelps (ed.), *Altruism, Morality and Economic Rheory*, Russell Sage Foundation, New York.

Chalkley, M. and Malcolmson, J.M. (1996), 'Contracts for the National Health Service', *Economic Journal*, 106, pp. 1691–701.

Croxson, B. (1999), *Organisational Costs in the New NHS. An introduction to the transaction costs and internal costs of delivering health care*, Office of Health Economics, London.

Deakin, S., Lane, C. and Wilkinson, F. (1997), 'Contract Law, Trust Relations, and Incentives for Co-operation: A comparative study', in S. Deakin and J. Michie (eds), *Contracts, Co-operation, and Competition. Studies in Economics, Management, and Law*, Oxford University Press, Oxford.

Department of Health and Social Security (1983), *NHS Management Inquiry (The Griffiths Report)*, HMSO, London.

Dixon, J. and Glennerster, H. (1995), 'What do we Know about Fundholding in General Practice?', *British Medical Journal*, 311, pp. 727–30.

Fisman, R. and Khanna, T. (1999), 'Is Trust a Historical Residue? Information Flows and Trust Levels', *Journal of Economic Behavior and Organization*, 38(1), pp. 79–92.

Flynn, R. and Williams, G. (eds) (1997), *Contracting for Health: Quasi-markets and the National Health Service*, Oxford University Press, Oxford.

Flynn, R., Williams, G. and Pickard, S. (1997), 'Quasi-markets and Quasi-trust: The social construction of contracts for community health services', in R. Flynn and G. Williams (eds), *Contracting for Health: Quasi-markets and the National Health Service*, Oxford University Press, Oxford.

Gambetta, D. (1998), *Trust: Making and breaking co-operative relations*, Blackwell, Oxford.

Glennerster, H., Matsaganis, M. and Owens, P. (1994), *Implementing GP Fundholding. Wild Card or Winning Hand?*, Open University Press, Buckingham.

Glennerster, H., Matsaganis, M., Owens, P. and Hancock, S. (1997), 'GP Fundholding. Wild Card or Winning Hand?', in R. Robinson and J. Le Grand (eds), *Evaluating the NHS Reforms*, King's Fund, London.

Goddard, M. and Mannion, R. (1998), 'From Competition to Co-operation: New economic relationships in the National Health Service', *Health Economics*, 7, pp. 105–19.

Hughes, D., Griffiths, L. and McHale, J.V. (1997), 'Do Quasi-markets Evolve? Institutional analysis and the NHS', *Cambridge Journal of Economics*, 21, pp. 259–76.

Keaney, M. and Lorimer, A.R. (1999), 'Clinical Effectiveness in the National Health Service in Scotland', *Journal of Economic Issues*, 33, pp. 117–40.

Kitchener, M. (1998), 'Quasi-market Transformation: An institutionalist approach to change in U.K. hospitals', *Public Administration*, 76, pp. 73–95.

Klein, R. (1995), *The New Oolitics of the NHS*, Longman, London.

Lyons, B. and Mehta, J. (1997a), 'Contracts, Opportunism and Trust: Self-interest and social orientation', *Cambridge Journal of Economics*, 21, pp. 239–57.

Lyons, B. and Mehta, J. (1997b), 'Private Sector Business Contracts: The text between the lines', in *Contracts, co-operation, and competition: studies in economics, management and law*, S. Deakin and J. Michie, (eds), Oxford University Press, Oxford.

Macneil, I.R. (1981), 'Economic analysis of contractual relations', in *The economic approach to law*, P. Burrows and C.G. Veljanovski, Butterworth, London.

McHale, J.V., D. Hughes and J. Griffiths (1997), 'Conceptualising contractual disputes in the National Health Service internal market', in *Contracts, co-operation, and competition: studies in economics, management and law*, S. Deakin and J. Michie, (eds), Oxford University Press, Oxford.

Montgomery, J. (1997), 'Control and restraint in National Health Service contracting', in S. Deakin and J. Michie (eds), *Contracts, Co-operation, and Competition. Studies in Economics, Management, and Law*, Oxford University Press, Oxford.

North, D.C. (1990), *Institutions, Institutional Change and Economic Performance*, Cambridge University Press, Cambridge.

Robinson, R. and Hayter, P. (1995), *Why do GPs Choose not to Apply for Fundholding?*, Occasional Paper, Institute for Health Policy Studies, University of Southampton.

Robinson, R. and Le Grand, J. (1994), *Markets and Contracting in Health Care*, Occasional Paper, Institute for Health Policy Studies, University of Southampton.

Sako, M. (1992), *Prices, Quality and Trust: Inter-firm relations in Britain and Japan*, Cambridge University Press, Cambridge.

Secretary of State for Health (1989), *Working for Patients* (Cmd 855), HMSO, London.

Secretary of State for Health (1997), *The New NHS: Modern and dependable* (Cmd 3807), HMSO, London.

Williamson, O.E. (1985), *The Economic Institutions of capitalism*, The Free Press, New York.

Williamson, O.E. (1993), 'Opportunism and its Critics', *Managerial and Decision Economics*, 14, pp. 97–107.

Zucker, L.G. (1986), 'The Production of Trust: Institutional sources of economic structure, 1840–1920', *Research in Organizational Behavior*, 8, pp. 53–111.

Chapter Fourteen

Explaining Variation in Grant Funding of Health Voluntary Organisations by Scottish Health Boards

Donald Routledge Coid and Iain Kinloch Crombie

Health Charities from the Victorian Era Onwards

During the nineteenth century capitalism, industrialisation and movement of population were potent forces of social change in Britain (Fraser, 1973). These social changes produced a substantial range of public health problems: infectious diseases, such as cholera and tuberculosis, and deficiency diseases such as scurvy and rickets, variously became sources of public concern. Although there was a substantial societal interest in charitable work, there was also a strand of public opinion that the provision of relief or care for people through governmental or non governmental means, encouraged idleness, improvidence or a lack of individual resourcefulness. One concept of charity was that it tended to degrade rather than uplift the recipient.

The public health movement was born at this time. One of its principal manifestations was the establishment of local and central government bureaucracies to deal with the problems. There was an acknowledgment that statutory organisations would play the major role in the amelioration of disease. The success of the statutory sector in dealing with health problems commenced mainly with the efforts of local government. Rates of infectious diseases came tumbling down, mainly as a result of a variety of environmental improvements relating to housing, water and food. School health programmes that followed in the early twentieth century – such as the availability of a preventive medical service and the provision of school milk – assisted in promoting the general health of the population. This could only have been effected by the governmental, statutory sector with its financial muscle on the one hand, and its ability to plan over wide areas of society on the other. During the second

Organisation Development in Health Care: Strategic Issues in Health Care Management, R.K. Rushmer, H.T.O. Davies, M. Tavakoli and M. Malek (eds), Ashgate Publishing Ltd, 2002.

half of the twentieth century the National Health Service became the main statutory organisation involved in health care. This was a major change as, prior to this time, many hospitals had been provided by charitable bodies. However the issues of access of all people to health care, the associated high costs, and the emphasis on high technology medicine were all aspects of social policy in which, it appeared, the non-statutory sector could not be much involved. Thus there was a continued effect of marginalisation of the non-governmental bodies from influence in health care.

The National Health Service and Twentieth Century Changes

The effect of the side-lining of the non-statutory sector was associated with ambivalent views in society of charitable enterprise. The voluntary organisations found themselves in a very lukewarm environment. For them, a damaging perspective prevailed, at the creation of the British National Health Service, that all necessary health care should be provided by the state. This implied that there was no need for charities: essential services would be provided by the state and funded via taxation. Furthermore, previous attempts to deliver health services via non-governmental bodies had not provided a safety net for the most needy groups of the population. The creation of the National Health Service was very popular, inspired partly by a belief that equity of health care provision would be more likely in the state run health service. The perceived need for charitable bodies was therefore diminished.

The reasons for the survival of health voluntary organisations, during the past 50 years, are obscure. There may a universal human need to be involved in welfare, particularly health care: the existence of a voluntary sector allows people without formal qualifications to participate in helping others. Even the process of supporting the voluntary sector financially may confer benefits at a psychological level. The placing of money in a collection tin for a charity is an action of solidarity with other people. It is less anonymous than provision of funds through a tax return and may be directed towards activities which the donor feels appropriate (Coid and Crombie, 1999). Notwithstanding the useful provision of a 'feel-good factor', the voluntary sector, overall, is also a serious economic player, employing many thousands of people and contributing 0.6 per cent of Britain's gross domestic product (Hems and Passey, 1996).

The Voluntary Sector and the Policy Environment

Despite the diminution in the influence of the voluntary sector over the last 50 years, there are thousands of such organisations active in Britain. Registers of the voluntary sector identify numerous bodies (Health Education Board for Scotland, 1998) which give support to people affected by even the most obscure diseases (Crombie and Coid, 2000). Despite the political difficulties, some have prospered. In fact half of the current national organisations have been started over the last 20 years (Bosanquet, 1995). Now, after many years in official wilderness, Voluntary Organisations are back on the political agenda. (Crombie and Coid, 2000) Their potential contribution has been highlighted in recent White Papers on the future of health care (Department of Health, 1999; Scottish Office Department of Health, 1998). In England, the Department of Health planned to spend £52 million in 1998–99 on the voluntary sector. Although this sum appears significant, it represents little more than £1 per head of population and is, proportionately, a small component of that country's health care expenditure. In Scotland, as in other UK countries, the influence of the voluntary sector has been recognised recently by a 'compact' between its representatives and government (Scottish Office, 1998), This identifies a range of shared values and acknowledges the respective priorities of the two sectors. But why should voluntary organisations be attracting this level of interest now? The answer may lie in the growing pressures on NHS resources and the consequent need to find ways to augment the delivery of care without increased cost. One way by which the National Health Service in Scotland (NHSiS) promotes activity of the voluntary sector is through the provision of funding, through a variety of channels. Amongst these is 'section 16B' funding, whereby health boards provide grants for voluntary bodies under the relevant section of the National Health Service (Scotland) Act 1978. Notwithstanding the political emphasis on the voluntary sector and an apparent interest by government in openness, details of this funding are obscure. For example, useful financial data are not available from readily available published sources such as health board annual reports or the annual report of the expenditure of the NHS in Scotland (Common Services Agency, Scottish Information and Statistics Division, 1997) Recently, the report of the Commission on the Future of the Voluntary Sector in Scotland (1997) called for increased accountability and transparency of public funding of this sector. This is an important issue as there are potentially thousands of organisations that may receive such funding. (Scottish Council for Voluntary Organisations (SCVO), 1996).

NHS and Voluntary Sector Fiscal Arrangements

In the absence of financial data in published format, a special study was undertaken in 1999 to identify the numbers and types of voluntary bodies supported by health board grants, throughout Scotland, and within individual health board areas. The principal results of this work are outlined in Table 14.1.

Table 14.1   Grant funding to voluntary organisations by health boards in Scotland, 1997–98

	Total health board grant expenditure (£)	Voluntary organisations funded (no.)	Per capita expenditure (£)	Expenditure per organisation funded (£)
Argyll and Clyde	38,620	21	0.09	1,839
Ayr and Arran	129,379	42	0.34	3,080
Borders	78,175	10	0.74	7,818
Dumfries and Galloway	88,704	22	0.60	4,032
Fife	491,210	23	1.41	21,357
Forth Valley	107,250	12	0.39	8,938
Grampian	641,200	28	1.21	22,900
Greater Glasgow	394,000	13	0.44	30,308
Highland	624,880	39	3.00	16,023
Lanarkshire	100,975	11	0.18	9,180
Lothian	21,150	6	0.03	3,525
Orkney	51,565	6	2.60	8,594
Shetland	0	0	n/a	n/a
Tayside	764,910	43	1.95	17,789
Western Isles	19,500	2	0.69	9,750
Scotland	3,551,518	278	0.69	12,979

n/a Shetland Health Board did not give grants to voluntary organisations in 1997/98 but paid for services from them on an *ad hoc* basis.

Of the 1,000 Scottish charities that have health care as their primary field of work (SCVO, 1996) and over 3,000 support organisations active in health (Health Education Board for Scotland, 1998) 278 received grants from health boards; thus the number who are financially supported is just a small minority of those eligible. Nationally the total grant commitment was £3,551,518, corresponding to 69p per head of population. While this is an important contribution to health care services provided by the voluntary sector, it represents less than 0.1 per cent of the revenue commitments of NHSiS

(Common Services Agency, Scottish Information and Statistics Division, 1997). The support for voluntary organisations by NHSiS grant expenditure is, relatively, a very modest part of the financial activity and suggests that financial partnership between the two bodies is a low priority.

The maximum number of health voluntary organisations supported by an individual health board was 43, by Tayside, a region in the east of Scotland whose population numbers 400,000. Individual grant expenditure of Scotland's 15 health boards on these bodies ranged from zero to £764,910. Of health boards that made grants to health voluntary bodies the range of expenditure per head of resident population was 9p to £3. The average individual grant made by health boards supporting voluntary organisations ranged from £1,839 to £30,308. The range of grant contributions of health boards to voluntary bodies was considerable. The highest per capita contributor, Highland Health Board, contributed at a rate 30 times that of the lowest, Lothian Health Board. The number of organisations supported also varies. Greater Glasgow Health Board, for example, funds just 13. Highland Health Board, serving about one-fifth of Glasgow's population makes grants to more than three times the number (43) of voluntary organisations. Glasgow's average contribution, £30,308 per organisation, is more than 15 times that of Argyll and Clyde's figure (£1,839).

Explanations of Fiscal Variance

The overall picture is therefore one of great variation from one geographical area to the other. Why should this be so? This variation certainly raises the question of whether distribution of funds is undertaken rationally or according to any national plan. The Scottish Executive supports volunteering in the National Health Service (Management Executive, 1998) but there is no explicit guidance on the amount of grant funding to be provided or the priorities care areas for spending on voluntary organisations. So there must be doubt whether money committed in this way purchases the range and depth of activity that the NHSiS wishes to support. Perhaps a more prescriptive range of policies from central government could lead to a more orderly approach. However current practice means that most grant funding decisions are left to local discretion. An argument in favour of this practice is that population needs for voluntary sector involvement in health care is assessed to be dramatically different according to geographical location. But there is there is little information on the activities and achievements of voluntary organisations in health related areas that would help make these judgments. Certainly there are pockets of deprivation throughout Scotland, where levels of public health need are greater. And in these areas interventions by the voluntary sector might be expected to be more needed to supplement the efforts of the statutory health services. If this is the case, again, there is little or no objective evidence of it in published literature.

Another possible explanation of variation might be due to the rurality of the different areas, where sociocultural differences and traditions might be expected to influence activities in the voluntary sector. However the health boards based on Scotland's 4 main cities (Tayside, Grampian, Greater Glasgow and Lothian) gave grants amounting to an average of 70p per head whereas the figure for the remaining health boards with a more rural population base was 69p per head. Furthermore, two of the three island boards, both with significantly isolated and rural communities were at the extremes of grant donation: Shetland Health Board (with its wealth garnered from the fishing and oil industries) giving nothing, while Orkney's per capita giving was one of the highest. The third islands' health board, Western Isles, gives 69 pence per head, the national average. Likewise, there was a weak relationship between the size of the board and the total grant disbursement (Spearman rank correlation = 0.26, p = 0.33 NS).

Do cultural variations play their part in explaining the fiscal phenomena? Scotland does not have a homogenous population. Affiliation to various organised religions is an important part of Scottish culture, particularly in the west and north of the country. Its religious traditions are associated with promotion of charitable organisations of all types. In the western isles, for example, active involvement with charitable organisations is particularly strong feature of the social fabric. On the other hand, charitable involvement in Shetland is more likely to be demonstrated by the giving of cash (rather then time) to voluntary organisations. The existence of the large numbers of charities throughout Scotland tends to increase the likelihood of them being favoured with funding. However voluntary organisations also greatly value their independence; this would be compromised by receipt of such funds.

A further reason to explain differing approaches is the lack of central policy guidance on the approaches to be taken for funding. While the election of the Blair government in 1997 has coincided with an expressed wish for more collaboration between the statutory and voluntary sectors (not just in health care), there has not been a corresponding emphasis on developing a relationship that incorporates specific fiscal responsibilities. The overall economic position favours restricted public spending. In this context health authorities see their primary responsibility in funding hospitals and primary care services, while the voluntary sector is an additional extra.

Finally for the NHSiS, which places a great premium on services provided by professional people, there is the question of the levels of expertise that exist in the voluntary sector. Unfortunately little or no information exists regarding its potential and there are few examples of health board employees with direct experience of working in the voluntary sector. Concurrently, some health voluntary organisations wish to operate in 'front line' clinical services. A BMJ editorial suggests that such voluntary organisations should be subjected to the same requirements to provide evidence of effectiveness as statutory services. (Crombie and Coid, 2000) However such data is even scarcer in the voluntary sector than elsewhere.

Conclusions

The 1997/98 national figure for grant funding, £3,551,518, identified by this study contrasts with the £8 million for 1996/97 estimated by the Scottish Council for Voluntary Organisations (SCVO) for the year 1994/5 (SCVO, 1997) based on a survey of 11 health boards. However, voluntary organisations may access NHS money through a variety of channels apart from direct grants. For instance, contractual payments and fees for specific items of service may be paid to charities that provide clinical services: private hospices – providing inpatient care for terminally-ill people – are an example. Other sources of NHS funding for voluntary organisations include NHS trusts that may have financial arrangements separate to those of their local health board. Fundholding general practitioners, until recently, have also been able to make their own arrangements with suppliers of services, including voluntary organisations. Other sources of money for the health voluntary organisations include European funding, donations from individuals and companies, legacies and the National Lottery.

The survival of the health voluntary organisations in a hostile environment during the twentieth century is remarkable. A spirit in the community seems to exist which prompts people to give their time and money to help others. Voluntary organisations are increasingly appreciated as bringing added value to state health services and the wider community. They allow people without formal qualifications to be involved health care. The relationship between them and the community should therefore be cherished. However this partnership is at present only modestly reflected in the fiscal support by the

NHSiS for the voluntary sector. This problem is not assisted by the obscurity of the rationale of expenditure nor the variability within Scotland. An uncoordinated approach disadvantages, at random, certain care groups according to their geographical location. The small contribution – relative to its overall fiscal commitments – of the NHSiS to the voluntary sector calls into question the equity of this programme. If it is to continue we suggest the impact of this funding is reviewed. What differences do these voluntary bodies make to the patients with which they serve? And to what extent is the expenditure good value for money?

Acknowledgments

We acknowledge the support of the Directors of Finance of the 15 Scottish Health Boards and their staff who assisted in providing data for this work. This project was supported by a grant from the Chief Scientist Office, Scottish Office Department of Health No: K/OPR/15/11 (3) DRC was supported by Tayside Health Board, Scotland, UK.

References

Bosanquet, N. (1995), 'An Introduction to the Voluntary Sector', *British Medical Journal*, 310, p. 1275.
Coid, D.R. and Crombie, I.K. (1999), 'Scotland's Health Service and the Voluntary Sector', *Scottish Medical Journal*, 44, p. 68.
Commission on the Future of the Voluntary Sector in Scotland (1997), *Head & Heart*, Scottish Council for Voluntary Organisations, Edinburgh.
Common Services Agency, Scottish Information and Statistics Division (1997), *Scottish Health Service Costs for Year Ended 31 March, 1997*, NHSiS, Edinburgh.
Crombie, I.K. and Coid, D.R. (2000), 'Voluntary Organisations: from Cinderella to White Knight?', *British Medical Journal*, 320, pp. 392–3.
Department of Health (1999), *Saving Lives; Our Healthier Nation*, The Stationery Office Limited, London.
Fraser, D. (1973), *The Evolution of the British Welfare State*, The Macmillan Press Ltd, London.
Health Education Board for Scotland (1998), *HEBS on CD*, HEBS, Edinburgh.
Hems, L. and Passey, A. (1996), *The UK Voluntary Sector Statistical Abstract*, NCVO Publications, London.
Management Executive (1998), *Guidance on Volunteering in the NHS*, Scottish Office, Edinburgh.
Scottish Council for Voluntary Organisations (1996), *The Scottish Voluntary Sector Almanac 1996*, SCVO, Edinburgh.

Scottish Council for Voluntary Organisations (1997), *Funding the Scottish Voluntary Sector*, SCVO, Edinburgh.

Scottish Office Department of Health (1998), *Working Together for a Healthier Scotland*, The Stationery Office Ltd, Edinburgh.

Scottish Office (1998), *The Scottish Compact: The principles underpinning the relationship between Government and the voluntary sector in Scotland*, The Stationery Office, Edinburgh.

Chapter Fifteen

Power as a Concept in the Evaluation of Telehealth

Sharon Levy, David A. Bradley, Moya J. Morison, Michael T. Swanston
and Susan Wilson

Introduction

The National Health Service (NHS) was created in 1948 to provide a unique, comprehensive and universal service free at the point of delivery and aimed at improving the health of the British population. Since its inception, the concept of a free service has been redefined and the ability of the system to respond to patients' holistic health care needs has been continually questioned. Societal changes which affected the NHS as well as other Western health care systems (European Commission, 1998) have led the UK government to re-evaluate its current health care strategy. Policy makers are seeking new ways to deliver, maintain and sustain the NHS while promoting effectiveness and efficiency as the means of reducing escalating health care costs.

At the onset of the new millennium health care providers are looking for innovative instruments propelled by modern technology, to allocate available resources, including time, money and organisational effort, to meet all the demands that compete for them. However, introducing new technology within care settings invariably constitutes a change to health care practices. The process of change involves people adopting new procedures and protocols to clinical work and there are likely to be those in favour of such changes and others who view the opportunity for change less positively. This chapter will describe the vision of a modern technology-led health service, as well as examining the concept of power as a change engine. The notion that change may be seen as a threat to the power of those who perceive the control of information as their territorial right will be explored while highlighting an apparent power paradox generated by technology in care. The authors argue that senior stakeholders who embrace seamless interagency collaboration, by

Organisation Development in Health Care: Strategic Issues in Health Care Management, R.K. Rushmer, H.T.O. Davies, M. Tavakoli and M. Malek (eds), Ashgate Publishing Ltd, 2002.

supporting and promoting information sharing through telehealth, have a pivotal role in the successful implementation of a new and modern NHS set to benefit all involved in care.

Telehealth: a Need-led Patient Centred Approach

The permanent tasks of formulating new strategic business objectives and developing alternative ways to meeting health care demands is a product of a dynamic and evolving process governed by politics. The current UK Labour government has confirmed in the White Paper *The New NHS: Modern, dependable* (DoH, 1997, p. 2) its commitment to maintaining a need led national health service by stating that '… access to health services is to be based on needs and needs alone'. However, Jones (1999) argues that the language of need used in current service planning is a need-based rhetoric, which supports a provider centric health care delivery environment. Telemedicine, on the other hand, has the potential to become an empowering engine for enabling a truly consumer-centric care delivery environment by facilitating self-care, ill-health prevention and the promotion of well-being. The realisation that deployment of such technology is an important tool in delivering a patient-led service has prompted the government to confirm that all health improvement programmes and associated strategies will need to demonstrate that telemedicine and telecare options have been considered (Stuart, 2000).

Telemedicine is not a single entity or form of intervention but rather a means by which to deliver a range of care processes. Definitions of tele-medicine abound, with most describing what is involved in the telemedicine process rather than providing a definition of what it is (Dodd, 1999). However, while recent discussions about the application of information and communication technology in health care have used the term telemedicine, it may be considered part of telehealth. This term, which appears to be increasingly favoured within the literature, represents more accurately the current philosophy of health care (Panahi and Shahtahmasebi, 1999). In essence, telehealth is the exchange of (health) care information where technology is used as an aid to overcome a spatial separation between providers and their clients. Such a broad definition also encompasses telecare, which is described as '… the remote or enhanced delivery of health and social support services to people in their own home by means of telecommunication and computer based system' (Barnes et al., 1998, p. 169). 'Telehealth' will be used throughout to encompass both telemedicine and telecare.

The intrinsic merit of telehealth derives from the ability to distribute and control the use of care services for maximal health gains. It is predicted therefore that incorporating such technology into the health service management structure will become a key component in future strategic planning of health care. Effective management aided by telehealth will manifest itself through a rational process whereby appropriate use of services and providers is encouraged by diminishing or removing barriers such as distance and time.

Moving into the Twenty-first Century: the 'New NHS'

Health care organisations throughout the world are perceived as evolving systems providing services according to population needs. However, changes such as the recent restructuring of services, through merging NHS trusts, health authorities and combining primary care practices into cooperatives, have left senior clinical staff disenchanted with yet another organisational change to services (McClenahan, 1999). Placing this current NHS reorganisation on a progressive chronological scale using Roberts' model (Roberts, 1992) highlights the fact that a significant difference, between this period and other restructuring phases, is at the heart of the strategic planning leading to the recent change.

Roberts' framework identifies three phases to structural changes within the UK health service and includes the *administrative period* (1948–74), the *planning period* (1974–84) and the *management period* (1984–90s). In the 1980s and early 1990s (management period) relatively few doctors and professional managers had the power and control over the access and utilisation of resources necessary to affect desired health outcomes. Such legitimate power (French and Raven, 1959), which stems from an individual's position within the organisation, gives managers exclusive access to invisible assets such as information. Legitimate power also provides access to distinctive networks which can be further used to the advantage of the power holder (Bond and Bond, 1994). The hierarchical management configuration within the NHS inspired by pro-market ideas established a power pyramid structure, where management control is placed at the apex. The marketing philosophy of the management period was to use interactions and efforts of staff in order to achieve service objectives channelled and coordinated through a market structure controlled via management. However, incorporating twenty-first century technology into this configuration highlights the fact that some of the processes mentioned could be carried out, at least in part, using electronic pathways.

The realisation that greater health care efficiencies could be achieved by using the latest technology has led the government to commit the NHS to undergo marked changes to the way services are to be provided in the future. A policy paper (NHS Executive, 1998) converts Labour's manifesto pledges to a strategy set to deliver:

• technically aided seamless care;
• on-line access to patients' records;
• public access to information and care through telemedicine.

Such commitment to an integrated telehealth solution and electronic information sharing represents a marked governmental policy shift from the previous 'information for managers' focused agenda (Gold and Wells, 1999). This vision of a new and modern NHS may therefore herald the beginning of a fourth structural change period to be added to Roberts' scale, the *integrated technical period*. In this new period all involved in care, including clients themselves, would have open (yet secured) access to relevant, timely and accurate information. The recent changes to health care services were therefore needed to provide a launching pad for the new NHS.

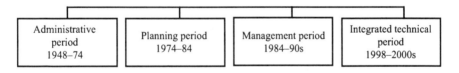

| Administrative period 1948–74 | Planning period 1974–84 | Management period 1984–90s | Integrated technical period 1998–2000s |

Figure 15.1 Structural changes within the NHS

Source: after Roberts, 1992.

The vision of a technically enhanced collaboration between different facets of the health care system is essential to help avoid the degradation of patient care as a result of poor availability of paper based records (Audit Commission, 1995). Yet collaboration in health care organisations is most often an association in which participants are rarely equal in status, prestige and power (Bond and Bond, 1994). The future use of telehealth may erode the 'old' hierarchical management structure as boundaries between health care settings become indistinct, but may also prove to be detrimental to care. Hornbey (1993) argues that set boundaries are an essential management tool, needed by professionals to define what they do and to set limits to what they are expected to do. Moreover, performing future care activity in a truly holistic way requires coordinated action to be taken by health, housing, informal and social care providers, leading to a need for an interface between a number of different boundaries to achieve a common purpose. Such an interface is encapsulated in ideas of 'multi-disciplinary health care collaboration' and the concept of 'partnership with clients' which are now widely accepted in care practice. Yet incorporating technology into these relationships is often viewed with misgivings. This despite the fact that all those involved in addressing health care needs depend upon each other for the quality and timeliness of necessary key data and information.

Understanding Change: the System Approach

Investigation of the impact of organisational change, where the inter-relationship between structure, people and technology is being sought, lends itself to a system analysis approach. This method, which is focused on the total organisation and the range of variables within it, identifies actual and potential problems in the function of systems. The aim of analysis is to outline intervention strategies that maximise efficient and effective system operation (Fawcett, 1989). Systems models view change as a concurrent element that is experienced by one part of the organisation yet affects all other parts of the system. Organisation system theories provide an explanation of behaviour in terms of the interaction of systems attempting to satisfy their organisational goal leading to homeostasis or equilibrium. However, these theories not only concentrate on the static rather than dynamic nature of organisational roles, but also disregard the diverse relationship held by different parts of the organisation regarding system's overall goal.

The open systems approach was developed in response to such criticism by presenting organisations as social organisms existing in relationship to the social environment. King's interacting systems framework is one example of such an open system model.

King (1981) describes a dynamic interacting model, which provides the basis for her conceptual framework for nursing. The unit of analysis in King's framework is human behaviour in a variety of social environments. Each individual is a personal system. Individuals interact in groups that represent interpersonal systems. Groups are formed as social systems in a community within society (King. 1995). For the purpose of this chapter, system units were renamed as: personal system (Individuals); interpersonal system (Interprofessional) and social system (Interagency).

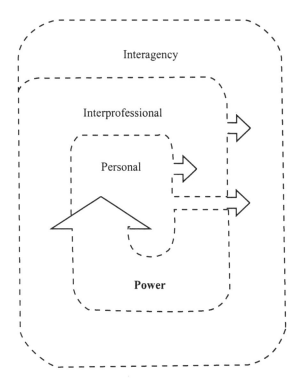

Figure 15.2 Power flow in an open integrated system

Source: after King, 1981.

King's framework is valuable, as it is not viewing human beings and their environment as separate detached entities but is rather concerned with human transactions (goal attainment) in different types of environments. Her model also encourages clients' participation in care and values the client's right to accept or reject the care offered by professionals (Fawcett, 1989). For these reasons, King's modified framework has been used to explore the system's anticipated power shift in the new integrated period and the role of information and technology in such a change.

The Concept of Power

King (1981) identifies the concept of power as relevant to the study of social systems by nurses. Power, in King's model, is viewed as a positive social factor. It is perceived as essential for the maintenance of balance and harmony within an organisation, essential for order in society and as beneficial for the achievement of goals (Sieloff 1995). A definition of power which fosters King's conceptual framework is provided by Hawks (1991, p. 760):

> Power was ... defined as the actual or potential ability or capacity to achieve objectives through an interpersonal process in which the goals and means to achieve the goals are mutually established and worked towards.

Such a view of power as a productive process that creates or facilitates the capacity to act is described as 'power to'. In contrast, 'power over' is associated with synonyms such as struggle for dominance, control, strength and authority. Regrettably, as noted by Hawks, power in the context of 'power over' is the focus of much of the literature on power in health care.

Gaston (1991) defines power as 'power over' when she states that:

> Power is control, influence or the ability to do or act. Power is the ability to make decisions and power is determining what those decisions will be in the first place. Power is having control of information.

A person's right to exercise 'power over' another person may stem from authority of position. In an ideal democratic society, equality ensures that authority resides in the position and not in the person. Claus and Bailey (1977) noted that although the power of management is legitimised by the organisation, management derives power not from command over people, but rather from assuming responsibility for carrying out functions and contributing to the organisational goals.

Michel Foucault's work within the field of medical sociology provides a useful analysis of the concept of power (Foucault, 1989). He asserts that health care professionals should not be seen as 'figures of domination' but rather as people through whom power passes (Turner, 1997). Power is a form of relationship which is diffused through the entire health care organisation, embedded in daily disciplinary practices, in technical processes and embodied in the health care culture. Power is not the possession of one group but a strategy, which is invested in and transmitted through all social groups.

Foucault also establishes a link between power and knowledge where he affirms that any extension of power involves an increase in knowledge and every elaboration of knowledge involves an increase in power (Turner, 1997). Senior clinicians in the current health care system have acquired specialist knowledge through their years of practice, enabling them to have an undisputed 'power to' facilitate learning and also 'power over' peers and patients. These professionals are being asked to do the impossible: store, update and retrieve on demand, the vast array of information and knowledge necessary to make high quality clinical decisions. There are now calls within the medical and nursing professions to engage new specialised information tools to enable fast and easy access by clinicians to relevant knowledge stores, to aid clinicians' unmet information needs and management tasks (Smith, 1996).

As noted earlier, the move away from dependence on inaccessible knowledge kept in the heads of senior clinicians to information sharing managed by technology, represents a marked shift in the balance of power within health care organisations. Furthermore, the use of telehealth could not only affect cost savings in health care administration but perhaps could also reduce one of the highest cost factors, that of specialised clinical manpower (Kahn, 1997). Telehealth, which facilitates the use of specialists in a remote consultative mode, could be further developed to include direct links to 'smart' decision support systems. By so doing, the technology will enable lesser trained providers to offer advice by following protocols and established metrics which are based on current knowledge. These technical specialists, who can be monitored by fewer senior clinical professionals, may provide accurate diagnosis or perform a clinical procedure by technical means at a much lower cost. Nevertheless, managers and policy makers have to ask themselves whether such 'mechanical' health care provision, whilst being cost effective, undermines the humanistic philosophy of a need led holistic care service.

Such revolutionary technology-led erosion of professionals' power echoes current trends in health care services. Much of what was once deemed to be the exclusive domain of the medical professional, is now being managed effectively and safely by nurse practitioners. In May 2000 the first Scottish nurse 'consultants' were appointed to provide expert advice to other nurses and midwives, and play a leading role in front-line patient care (Scottish Executive, 2000). These consultants will be able to run clinics, offer advice, prescribe medication and have their own patients' in a similar way to their medically trained colleagues. Moreover, many patients nowadays prefer to use complementary therapies as an alternative to seeking the help of conventional health care practitioners. The most rigorous UK survey of complementary medicine use estimated that, in 1993, 33 per cent of the population had used some form of alternative therapy administered, in the majority of cases, by a nonmember of the primary health care team (Zollman and Vickers, 1999).

This move away from traditional delivery of health care may be due in part to the drive down the technological road of 'high tech' medicine. A drive which has resulted in a decrease of personal holistic care given to patients. The growth in alternative health care could also be attributed to people asserting themselves as consumers of health care, exercising choice and demanding value for money spent on private treatments and care. The growing willingness to pay also indicates users' disenchantment with the 'cradle to grave' service promise, leading them to question whether health care service cannot or will not deliver their perceived right for lifelong care.

Consumerism as a philosophy in health care, where service users are seen as customers of care, places responsibility for health on informed individuals by giving them the power to act in their own best interest. Health care professionals who argue that patients' interests can only be defined and assessed by those with the 'right' knowledge while disregarding patients' right to autonomy, self-determination and full involvement in their care, may be seen as guarding against a power shift.

The Technological Paradox

Fifty years ago health care could be said to be about patients' dependency. There was an implicit expectation of patients to surrender all powers to a clinical 'Big Brother' while in institutional care. It may be argued that health care professionals have had too much power and influence over the lives of lay people, diminishing their capacity for autonomy in dealing with their own health care needs (Lupton, 1997). Today's telehealth approach, echoing a general trend in health care management, is intended to empower patients, deliver services in a more efficient way and bridge traditional boundaries in a truly holistic and patient-centred way.

Empowerment is defined as:

> ... a social process of recognising, promoting and enhancing peoples' abilities to meet their own needs, solve their own problems and mobilise the necessary resources to feel in control of their own lives (Gibson, 1991, p. 355).

Telehealth facilitates this process by providing choice through information delivered in a more convenient and accessible manner. Telehealth can provide clients with information tailored to their needs as part of an interactive digital capability which includes up-to-date health care information detailing treatment options and the outcome of any potential intervention. This information can be accessed anonymously at home where patients have the time to reflect and consider the best course of action. In effect the government supports such a vision by reiterating that better care and improved health for everyone depends on the availability of good information, accessible when and where it is needed (NHS Executive, 1998).

However, Sandellowski (1999, p. 13) notes that

> ... technological innovation, in addition to creating new human arrangements and possibilities, often serves only to reinforce existing sociocultural practices, norms and values.

The implications of such a statement can be appreciated if one considers the fact that senior clinicians (medical doctors) are most likely to be involved in the set-up of health care technical innovations (Gerrard et al., 1999). Moreover, health care managers (who are responsible for finance) are increasingly likely to take a lead role in determining which technology is employed and how it is introduced within the organisation. It is further suggested that new health care technology which is intended to empower patients, often merely maintains power differentials between physicians and their clients by 'muting' the voices of patients (Forsythe, 1996). The clinical 'Big Brother', armed with the latest technology has the means to track patients, access their information and in effect silence those who oppose such control over their life. Telehealth, besides providing a means of efficient management of resources, may shift the reliance on communication with patients to reliance on data and information about patients. Sandellowski argues that technology advancement may alter the focus of care from 'high touch' to 'high tech' practice, whereby the effectiveness of a warm and friendly interaction between a person who experiences ill health and a competent provider who can use his/her power in a therapeutic manner is lost.

Sandellowski's observation implies that the failure of technological innovations to impact on 'power to' may promote 'power over' whereby the pre-existing culture is being reinforced through the use of technology. Clinicians she argues, may perceive accurate, scientific, 'real time' data as a high added-value tool for disease management, while disregarding the person who suffers from the disease and his/her holistic needs. The emergence of a consumer orientated health care service, which is a prominent feature within the forth structural period of the NHS, may go in some way to ensuring an even playing field in health care or may even shift 'power over' to consumers. Consumerists maintain that information and choice are easily mixed up but that there can be information without choice, whereas there cannot be choice without information. Patients can share the decision-making process regarding their care only if they are given enough relevant information which is aimed at their level of understanding (Williamson, 1992).

Consumers of health care may use telehealth to control and manage their own needs by accessing information and on-line services directly, reducing the reliance on consultation with clinicians to a minimum. Professional care, according to this vision, will function as the support to a technical system that enables self care (Smith, 1997). The apparent technological paradox is that the new innovation may serve as a tool which shifts the 'power over' from professionals to their perceived customers while losing along the way the ability to gain from clinician's 'power to' facilitate appropriate care. Richard (1988) argues that the right care for most people who feel unwell is neither investigation nor treatment, but rather an explanation and reassurance given by a trusted clinician. He claims that

> ... [D]octors may become biological, structural, mechanical and electrical engineers called in to fix a faulty part. The doctor–patient relationship of trust and understanding [may] become a memory of the past.

King's conceptual framework, which serves as a model for the shared decision making process, could lead the way to solving such a power paradox by presenting telehealth as the means by which to attain goals and foster brotherhood (social cohesion) rather than enacting a powerful technically-able 'Big Brother'. Telehealth is not just a medical aid or a clinical information system but an information service which fosters the notion of information as a human right and a tool for self empowerment. King's framework reiterates that individuals, who are perceived as social beings both rational and sentient, have the right to:

- have knowledge about themselves;
- participate in decisions that influence their life, their health and community services; and
- accept or reject health care.

According to this framework health care professionals, have a responsibility to share information that can help individuals make informed decisions about their health care (King, 1981).

King notes that the capacity to interact meaningfully is a fundamental human quality which enables individuals to work in partnership to achieve a common goal. Goal orientated interaction, as represented in her model, is a product of three dynamic and interacting systems which maintain a collaborative balance of power. As mentioned earlier, within *personal systems* 'power to' is seen as a cornerstone for a therapeutic relationship and telehealth may be used as a medium for communication and sharing of information on which agreed plan of *action* is developed. *Interprofessional interaction* is the electronic sharing of resources for action and knowledge gained through such action. The *interagency* system which serves as the outer layer of the model represents the nourishing environment in which action and interaction take place. Technically aided collaboration, where power is seen as a shared commodity, ensures an optimal setting for health care *transaction* leading to goal attainment.

It is argued that managers within the interagency system hold the key to the successful implementation of change generated by telehealth. Individuals who are responsible for the strategic management of their organisations must harness technology to further collaborations between the various agencies, including clients and carers, so that planned care achieves agreed goals. Failing to accept such power sharing in a system which embraces technological advances, may lead to the demise of a service which was created to protect the most vulnerable in society.

Conclusion

The political push for a modern health care service presents technology as a panacea for what is perceived to be inadequate health care resource provision. This chapter has examined some of the issues impacting on a new health care service which uses telehealth in achieving health gains and maintenance of well being. Using King's modified open systems model, it was highlighted that the full utilisation of the potential inherent in an innovation such as telehealth, depends on a system's equilibrium. 'Power to' which is used throughout the system at all levels, is suggested as a key to change management leading to a balanced technically able health care service of the future.

Telehealth, which provides the means and medium for knowledge sharing and open communication, must be itself perceived by users as powerless. In this way a power paradox, whereby users or providers are using the access to information and knowledge as 'power over', is resolved. Nil 'power currency' attributed to telehealth can only be achieved by ensuring that all involved in care have full access to adequate training. Trained health care staff and their clients will become more than just willing users but partners in operating technology to its full potential.

The current political push for technology in health care fails to foster a framework for managing an organisational change as presented in this chapter. Imposing technology into a human-based service, without proper consideration to the system's needs, may hinder efforts to create a new and modern health service of the twenty-first century.

References

Audit Commission (1995), *Setting the Records Straight: A study of hospital medical records*, Audit Commission, London.

Barnes, N.M., Edwards, N.H., Rose, D.A.D., and Garner, P. (1998), 'Lifestyle Monitoring – Technology for Supported Independence', *IEE Computing and Control Engineering Journal*, 9(4), pp. 169–74.

Bond, J. and Bond, S. (1994), *Sociology and Health Care*, 2nd edn, Churchill Livingston, Edinburgh.

Claus, K. and Bailey, J. (1977), *Power and Influence in Health Care*, C.V. Mosby Company, Saint Louis.

Dodd, B. (1999), 'Telemedicine: Curse or blessing?', *The British Journal of Healthcare Computing & Information Management,* 16(5), pp. 22–4.

Department of Health (DoH) (1997), *The New NHS: Modern, dependable*, The Stationery Office, London.

European Commission, Telematics Applications Programme (1998), *Report of the Strategic Requirements Board*, available at URL: http://www2.echo.lu/telematics/health/health.html (accessed 14 June 1999).

Fawcett, J. (1989), *Analysis and Evaluation of Conceptual Models of Nursing*, 2nd edn, F.A Davis Company, Philadelphia.

Forsythe, D. (1996), 'New Bottles, Old wine: Hidden cultural assumption in a computerized explanation system for migraine sufferers', *Medical Anthropology Quarterly*, 10, pp. 551–74.

Foucault, M. (1989), *The Birth of the Clinic: An archaeology of medical perception*, Routledge, London.

French, J.R.P. and Raven, B.H. (1959), 'The Bases of Social Power', in D. Cartwright (ed.), *Group Dynamics: Research and Theory*, University of Michigan Press, Michigan, pp. 150–67.

Gaston, C. (1991), 'The Politics of Nursing Information Systems and Resource Allocation', in E.J.S. Hovenga (ed.), *Nursing Informatics '91: proceedings of the Fourth International Conference*, Springer-Verlag, New York.

Gerrard, L., Maclean, J.R., Grant, A., Lowis, A., Wilcock, S., Page, G., Brebner, J., and Bower, J. (1999), *The Human Resource Implications for the Nursing Profession in Developing Telemedicine within the NHS*, Health Service Research Unit University of Aberdeen, Aberdeen.

Gibson, C. (1991), 'A Concept Analysis of Empowerment', *Journal of Advanced Nursing*, 16, pp. 354–61.

Gold, G. and Wells, H. (1999), *Preserving Confidentiality in the Age of Electronic Records*, proceedings of the annual conference of the Primary Health Care Specialist Group of the British Computing Society, Cambridge, available at URL: http://www.schin.ncl.ac.uk/phcsg/conferences/Cambridge1999/camb99-05.htm (accessed 2 February 2000).

Hawks, J. (1991), 'Power: A concept analysis', *Journal of Advanced Nursing*, 16, pp. 754–62.

Hornbey, S. (1993), *Collaborative Care: Interprofessional, interagency, and interpersonal*, Blackwell Scientific Publications, Oxford.

Jones, I.R. (1999), *Professional Power and the Need for Health Care*, Ashgate Publishing Ltd, Aldershot.

Kahn, G. (1997), *Digital Interactive Media and the Health Care Balance of Power*, Lawrence Erlbaum Associates, New Jersey.

King, I. (1981), *A Theory for Nursing. Systems, Concepts, Process*, John Wiley & Sons, New York.

King, I. (1995), *A Systems Framework for Nursing*, Sage Publications, California.

Lupton, D. (1997), 'Foucault and the Medicalisation Critique', in A. Petersen and R. Bunton (eds), *Foucault, Health and Medicine*, Routledge, London, pp. 94–110.

McClenahan, J. (1999), 'Apart at the seams', *Health Service Journal*, 104(5681), pp. 22–3.

NHS Executive (1998), *Information for Health: An information strategy for the modern NHS 1998–2005*, Department of Health, London.

Panahi, G.R. and Shahtahmasebi, S. (1999), 'The Implication of Telemedicine for Nursing', *Professional Nurse*, 14(2), pp. 835–8.

Richard, P. (1988), *Doctors, the NHS and 21st Century*, BBC Education on-line, available at URL: http://www.bbc.co.uk/education/health/dal/future.shtml (accessed 14 January 2000).

Roberts, J. (1992), 'The Drama of the NHS', *Critical Public Health*, 3(1), 3, pp. 5–41.

Sandellowski, M. (1999), 'Culture, Conceptive Technology, and Nursing', *International Journal of Nursing Studies*, 36, pp. 13–20.

Scottish Executive (2000), press releases May 2000: 'First Scottish "Super Nurses" Appointed', available at URL: http://www.scotland.gov.uk/news/2000/05/se1438.asp (accessed 30 August 2000).

Sieloff, C. (1995), *Development of a Theory of Departmental Power*, Sage Publications, California.

Smith, R. (1996), 'What Clinical Information do Doctors Need?' *British Medical Journal*, 313, pp. 1062–8.

Smith, R. (1997), 'The Future of Healthcare Systems', *British Medical Journal*, 314(7093), pp. 1495–9.

Stuart, G. (2000), *House of Commons Hansard Debates for 4 May 2000 (pt 33): The parliamentary under-secretary of state for Health: Telemedicine*, available at URL: http://www.parliament.the-stationery-office.co.uk/pa/cm199900/cmhansrd/cm000504/debtext/00504-33.htm (accessed 29 May 2000).

Turner, S.T. (1997), 'From Governmentality to Risk: Some reflection on Foucault's contribution to medical sociology', in A. Petersen and R. Bunton (eds), *Foucault: Health and medicine*, Routledge, London.

Williamson, C. (1992), *Whose Standards? Consumer and Professional Standards in Health Care*, Open University Press, Buckingham.

Zolman, C. and Vickers, A. (1999), 'Users and Practitioners of Complementary Medicine' *British Medical Journal*, 319, pp. 836–8.

List of Contributors

J. Alleyne
Principal Lecturer, Health Care and Nursing Management, School of Health, Biological, and Environmental Sciences, Middlesex University

Lawrence Benson
Lecturer, Division of Health Care Studies, School of Health Studies, University of Bradford

David A. Bradley
School of Science and Engineering, University of Abertay, Dundee

Helen Bussell
Senior Lecturer in Marketing, School of Business and Management, University of Teesside

Andrew Chalmers
Faculty of Medicine, University of British Columbia

Donald Routledge Coid
Honorary Senior Lecturer, Department of Epidemiology and Public Health, Ninewells Hospital and Medical School

Iain Kinloch Crombie
Department of Epidemiology and Public Health, Ninewells Hospital and Medical School, Dundee

Lisa Cunnington
Project Co-ordinator, South Tees Hospital

Graeme Currie
University of Nottingham Business School, Jubilee Campus

Organisation Development in Health Care: Strategic Issues in Health Care Management, R.K. Rushmer, H.T.O. Davies, M. Tavakoli and M. Malek (eds), Ashgate Publishing Ltd, 2002.

Terry Downes	Clinical Services Manager, South Birmingham Mental Health NHS Trust, Older Adult Directorate
Irene Goldstone	British Columbia Centre for Excellence in HIV/AIDS and School of Nursing, University of British Columbia
Peter Granger	Faculty of Medicine, University of British Columbia and Three Bridges Community Health Centre
Dave Haran	Senior Lecturer, Health Sector Reform Work Programme, Liverpool School of Tropical Medicine
Carol Hornsby	South Tees Acute NHS Trust
M.O. Jumaa	Principal Lecturer, Health Care and Nursing Management, School of Health, Biological, and Environmental Sciences, Middlesex University
John Kimberly	INSEAD, Healthcare Management Initiative, Fontainebleau, France
Leonard Lerer	INSEAD, Healthcare Management Initiative, Fontainebleau, France
Sharon Levy	School of Science and Engineering, University of Abertay, Dundee,
Neil Marr	Editor, BeWrite
Robert Martel	Providence Health Care and School of Social Work and Family Studies, University of British Columbia

Sharon McKinnon	Faculty of Pharmaceutical Sciences, University of British Columbia
Robert McMaster	Department of Economics, University of Aberdeen
Moya J. Morison	School of Social and Health Sciences, University of Abertay, Dundee
Dorothy Noble	Regional Nursing Officer, QARANC
Oliver Nyumbu	Director, Caret Consulting Ltd, Birmingham
Brian O'Neill	School of Social Work and Family Studies, University of British Columbia
Paula Palmer	Occupational Psychologist , NHS Staff College Wales
Julia Parker	OD Manager, Dundee Primary Care NHS Trust, Ashludie Hospital, Monifieth
Paul Perchal	AIDS Vancouver
Sheila Phillips	Development Manager, Dundee LHCC, Liff Hospital
Sue Phillips	Quality Manager, MHSOA, South Birmingham Mental Health NHS Trust
Stephen Procter	Department of Management, University of St Andrews
Zillyham Rojas	Director of Central American Institute for Health, Costa Rica
Rosemary K. Rushmer	Director of the Teamwork Research Centre, University of Abertay, Dundee

Jayne Sayers	Training Co-ordinator, Primary Care Services for Older Adults, Mental Health Services of Salford NHS Trust
Steven Simoens	Health Economics Research Unit, University of Aberdeen
Lisa Sinclair	Pursglove Management Centre
Michael T. Swanston	School of Social and Health Sciences, University of Abertay, Dundee
Brian Toner	Service Director, MHSOA, South Birmingham Mental Health NHS Trust
Stephanie Williams	Director Qualifications and Research, NHS Staff College Wales and Lecturer, Health Service Management, University of Wales College of Medicine
Susan Wilson	Tayside Primary Care NHS Trust, Dundee
Gillian Wright	Department of Strategic Management, John Moores University Liverpool
Anne Wyness	School of Nursing, University of British Columbia